# FRUITFUL

# FRUITFUL

## A Study of the Fruit of the Spirit

GWENDOLYN HARMON

Learning Ladyhood Press

Copyright © 2022 by Gwendolyn Harmon

Cover photo by Rebecca Harmon, used by permission.

All rights reserved. No part of this book may be reproduced in any manner whatsoever without written permission except in the case of brief quotations embodied in critical articles and reviews.

First Printing, 2022

# Contents

1. Works, Grace, and the Gospel — 1
2. Love — 6
3. Joy — 11
4. Peace — 24
5. Longsuffering — 36
6. Gentleness — 47
7. Goodness — 54
8. Faith — 68
9. Meekness — 79
10. Temperance — 90

# 1

# Works, Grace, and the Gospel

It is important in studying any passage of Scripture to begin with an understanding of the context in which it has been placed. The two verses listing the fruit of the Spirit do not exist in a vacuum, so it is crucial to our study of these qualities to first look at the book of Galatians as a whole.

The book of Galatians was written by Paul (through the inspiration of the Holy Spirit) to the believers in Galatia. Paul wrote this particular epistle because the Galatian believers had fallen prey to false teaching regarding the relationship of works to salvation. Essentially, Paul presents the Galatians with a truth and its two extremes.

The first four and a half chapters give a detailed argument against works-based salvation, specifically the false doctrine of the Judaizers, who wanted to add adherence to the Old Testament law as a requirement for salvation. It is clear from this first part of Galatians, as well as Scripture as a whole, that the Gospel is of grace, by faith, as Ephesians 2:8-9 states:

*"For by grace are ye saved through faith; and that not of yourselves: it is the gift of God: not of works, lest any man should boast."*

The Galatian believers had mixed the truth of the gospel with a lie. After having placed their trust in Christ's finished work of redemption as full payment for their sin, they were now persuaded that Christ's sacrifice was not enough: it was up to them to make up the difference by keeping the Old Testament law.

There are several problems with this. The first is that salvation by the law would necessarily demand that the law be kept perfectly—it only takes one sin to bring the death sentence of sin upon a soul. Romans 3:23 tells us that *"all have sinned and come short of the glory of God,"* and you and I can attest to the truth of that statement in our own lives. Each of us has broken at least one of God's laws, and no quantity of good deeds can change that fact in the sight of God.

The next problem with the philosophy of grace-plus-law is that keeping the law was never God's salvation plan to begin with. Galatians 2:15-16 addresses this point:

*"We who are Jews by nature, and not sinners of the Gentiles, Knowing that a man is not justified by the works of the law, but by the faith of Jesus Christ, even we have believed in Jesus Christ, that we might be justified by the faith of Christ, and not by the works of the law: for by the works of the law shall no flesh be justified."*

Paul here is describing the prideful way the Jewish Christians were hanging onto certain aspects of the law (and not very consistently, either,) while looking down on the Gentile Christians as "sinners" or inferior because they did not do likewise. This passage joins many other clear statements in Scripture which show us that the gospel isn't about anything we *do*: it's about what Christ has *already done*.

A good summary of Paul's argument against the false doctrine of works-based salvation is found in the first verse of chapter 5, which says,

*"Stand fast therefore in the liberty wherewith Christ hath made us free, and be not entangled again with the yoke of bondage."*

Paul goes on to explain that faith in the law for salvation *negates* faith in Christ: if you can save yourself under the law, why did Christ come? As Paul puts it,

*"Christ is become of no effect unto you, whosoever of you are justified by the law; ye are fallen from grace." (5:4)*

He isn't saying that these Christians have lost their salvation because they are trying to keep the law: instead, he is pointing out that faith in the law and faith in Christ (salvation by grace) are incompatible. If one is true, the other is necessarily false.

So, now that Paul has shown the law to be fundamentally ineffective in terms of salvation, it can be completely discarded and we can just do what we want, right?

Not at all.

From 5:13 on, Paul addresses another side of the issue, wisely acknowledging the tendency of mankind to swing from one extreme to the other.

*"For, brethren, ye have been called unto liberty; only use not liberty for an occasion to the flesh, but by love serve one another. For all the law is fulfilled in one word, even this; Thou shalt love thy neighbor as thyself." (5:13-14)*

While maintaining the truth of salvation by faith through grace, Paul turns our attention to the true role of the law in the life of the Christian; and that's where the fruit of the Spirit comes in.

There is a delicate tightrope of truth between works salvation and total denial of the relevancy of doing right in the Christian life. Salvation by faith through grace is not an isolated event. It is the glorious moment when the Holy Spirit of God comes to dwell in the heart of the believer, nevermore to leave. The work of the Holy Spirit in our lives is the source of any true "good works" we do, hence Paul's call to walk in the Spirit:

*"This I say then, Walk in the Spirit, and ye shall not fulfil the lust of the flesh. For the flesh lusteth against the Spirit, and the Spirit against the flesh: and these are contrary the one to the other: so that ye cannot do the things that ye would. But if ye are led of the Spirit, ye are not under the law."* (5:16-18)

You see, we are prone to give in to the lusts of the flesh, to do what feels good at the moment; but that is not the will of God for the Christian. He gives us the Holy Spirit so that we might live according to His will, doing those things that He says are right.

Walking in the Spirit will end up looking a lot like keeping the law. That's why Paul makes a point of stating that those who walk in the Spirit are not under the law. We are not bound to keep its every statute on pain of eternal death in hell.

Instead, we follow Jesus' example through the Holy Spirit's leading, seeking to *"do always those things that please Him."* (John 8:29)

Believers in works-based salvation do good because they *have* to, but the Spirit-led, saved-by-grace believer does good because he or she *wants to*. That is the true relationship of works to salvation: they are the result, not the cause.

The intersection of works, grace, and the Gospel is life in the Spirit, which is Paul's focus throughout the rest of the book of Galatians. It is in this section on Spirit-filled living that we find the fruit of the Spirit listed. This is a significant fact, because the fruit of the Spirit is not a list of things we *do*, or qualities we need to somehow work up inside us: they are instead the natural outpouring of the Spirit of God flowing through us as we yield to Him.

As we begin this look at the qualities of the fruit of the Spirit, remember that it's not about us somehow doing better: it's about God working in and through us. When we demonstrate the qualities of the fruit of the Spirit, it is solely because we are allowing the Spirit to guide our actions and attitudes. As in all things, it's not about us, it's about God.

> *"Faithful is He that calleth you, who also will do it." (1 Thessalonians 5:24)*

# 2

# Love

*"But the fruit of the Spirit is love, joy, peace, longsuffering, gentleness, goodness, faith, Meekness, temperance: against such there is no law."*
*Galatians 5:22-23*

This list of traits that flow out of a Spirit-filled Christian begins with the word *love*. Love is a somewhat nebulous and relative term in our modern society, used towards anything from our favorite food to a family member, spouse, or child. But what does the Bible mean when it says that the fruit of the Spirit is love?

This is a case where a look at the original Greek word gives us a fuller understanding of what is meant. The Greek word used is *Agape*, a very specific word in the Greek language. John Phillips explains,

"Agape is the spontaneous love, love irrespective of 'rights.' It is the word commonly used in the New Testament to describe the matchless love of God."*

In fact, *agape* is the word translated as "charity" throughout the New Testament. It appears in Romans 5:8, which says,

*"But God commendeth His love toward us, in that, while we were yet sinners, Christ died for us."*

The verb form of this same word is used in Ephesians 5:25.

*"Husbands, love your wives, even as Christ also loved the church, and gave Himself for it"*

Agape love is the self-sacrificing love Christ has for sinners, the love that moved Him to willingly bear the pain and suffering of the cross, rejoicing in the redemption it would accomplish on behalf of His beloved ones.

This kind of love is an *attribute* of God, a key element of who He is. 1 John 4:8 tells us this when it states that God *is* love. God doesn't just show or feel love, He *is* love. We can no more separate God from the love that defines Him than we can His holiness, omnipotence, justice, or mercy. The attributes of God are not individual pieces of His character, they are facets of the glorious whole of His nature.

There are some attributes God cannot share with His human creatures, such as His omnipotence, omnipresence, and omniscience. However, there are some attributes He calls us to reflect through the power of the Holy Spirit working in and through us. Theologians call these "sharable" attributes *communicable*. Love is one of those communicable attributes which God desires to share with us.

Now, all this theological knowledge is good, but you may be asking, *So how do I love as God does?* We love, quite simply, by obeying God. Note the following passages:

*"Owe no man any thing, but to love one another: for He that loveth another hath fulfilled the law. For this, Thou shalt not commit adultery, Thou*

shalt not kill, Thou shalt not steal, Thou shalt not bear false witness, Thou shalt not covet; and if there be any other commandment, it is briefly comprehended in this saying, namely, Thou shalt love thy neighbor as thyself. Love worketh no ill to his neighbour: therefore love is the fulfilling of the law." Romans 13:8-10

"But whoso keepeth His word, in him verily is the love of God perfected: hereby know we that we are in Him." (1 John 4:5)

These two passages clearly teach that we know that we are in Christ when we show His love to others, and that this *agape* love is shown by obedience to God's commands. This is partly why love is considered by many to be the root of all the other characteristics listed as the fruit of the Spirit.

If you were to compare the description of charity (*agape* love) in 1 Corinthians 13 with the other characteristics of the fruit of the Spirit in Galatians 5:22, you would see quite a bit of overlap. Many of the descriptions of charity could easily be used to define or describe the other characteristics of the fruit of the Spirit. At the beginning of 1 Corinthians 13, just before the description of charity, we find these verses:

"Though I speak with the tongues of men and of angels, and have not charity, I am become as sounding brass, or a tinkling cymbal. And though I have the gift of prophecy, and understand all mysteries, and all knowledge; and though I have all faith, so that I could remove mountains, and have not charity, I am nothing. And though I bestow all my goods to feed the poor, and though I give my body to be burned, and have not charity, it profiteth me nothing." (vv.1-3)

You see, *agape* love is essential to anything we "do" in our Christian walk. Just as we cannot separate God's other attributes from His love, so the Christian cannot separate joy, peace, longsuffering, gentleness, goodness, faith, meekness, or temperance from love. A heart of Christ-like love is the foundation upon which all the other characteristics are built.

What will it look like to love as God loves? Our obedience to the Holy Spirit will cause us to show love to others in practical ways. The description of charity from 1 Corinthians 13 is a good passage to use to check our thoughts, feelings, attitudes, and actions and see if we are allowing the Holy Spirit to bring forth fruit in our hearts and lives.

*"Charity suffereth long, and is kind; charity envieth not; charity vaunteth not itself, is not puffed up, Doth not behave itself unseemly, seeketh not her own, is not easily provoked, thinketh no evil; rejoiceth not in iniquity, but rejoiceth in the truth; Beareth all things, believeth all things, hopeth all things, endureth all things. Charity never faileth." (vv.4-8a)*

If you're at all like me, you found at least a few things on that list that do not characterize your life. The important thing to remember about these characteristics is that we do not have to make them happen ourselves: we simply yield to the Holy Spirit, and He gives us the power to obey. We can only love as God loves by yielding to the Spirit.

It is also important to remember that each moment is a new opportunity to obey. We always have the option of growing in Christ, of loving better, of yielding more to the Holy Spirit. That is why Paul said,

*"And this I pray, that your love may abound yet more and more in knowledge and in all judgement; That ye may approve things that are excellent; that ye may be sincere and without offence till the day of Christ; being filled with the fruits of righteousness, which are by Jesus Christ, unto the glory and praise of God." (Philippians 1:9-11)*

Love, like the rest of the fruit of the Spirit, can grow, abound, and fill our hearts and lives—if we will let it!

*Phillips, John *Exploring Galatians: an Expository Commentary*. Kregel publications: Grand Rapids 2004.

## 3

# Joy

*"But the fruit of the Spirit is love, joy, peace, longsuffering, gentleness, goodness, faith, Meekness, temperance: against such there is no law."*
*Galatians 5:22-23*

It's amazing how much theology there is in the children's songs we sang in Sunday school or with our own children. Here is one I remember singing often as a child:

"I've got joy, down in my heart,
Deep, deep down in my heart!
J-O-Y, down in my heart,
Deep, deep down in my heart!
Jesus gave it to me
And nothing can destroy it!
I've got joy, down in my heart,
Deep, deep down in my heart!"

Despite the simple and repetitive nature of the lyrics, this little song contains a sometimes uncomfortable truth from Scripture. It says that the joy Jesus gives is indestructible. Think about that for a moment. Now read what Jesus says in John 15:11:

> "These things have I spoken unto you, that My joy might remain in you, and that your joy might be full."

For the saved in Christ, our joy is the joy of Christ dispensed to us by the Holy Spirit. As Jesus said, our joy is to *remain*. That word can also mean to stay, to be present, to continue, abide, dwell, or endure. Once joy is given, God means it to stay put.

But we don't always *feel* joyful, do we? You may be reading this with a heart that feels as if all the joy has been sapped out of it. What do we do with the reality of joyless seasons, when Jesus Himself said that His joy was to remain?

We trust that what God's Word says is true.

Remember that the fruit of the Spirit is a list of things that will fill and overflow our hearts as we walk in the Spirit. Just as love never fails (1 Corinthians 13:8) yet we will fail to love if we are letting our flesh control us, so the joy that is to remain will be conspicuously absent if we are not in submission to the Holy Spirit.

So, joyless reader, take heart! You cannot manufacture joy or somehow work it up inside you, but you can get close to God and let the Holy Spirit fill you with the joy that remains.

## RESTORING JOY

There is, however, a time *not* to be joyful. James 4:8-10 was written to a group of Christians who had been chasing after worldly things, finding themselves aligned with the world instead of with God. James has some very strong words for them, pointing out that their lust after worldly things is like adultery, putting them at enmity with God. That is a very serious position to be in, but James does not leave them helpless. He tells them how to get back to a right relationship with God:

*"Draw nigh to God, and He will draw nigh to you. Cleanse your hands, ye sinners, and purify your hearts, ye double-minded. Be afflicted, and mourn, and weep: let your laughter be turned to mourning, and your joy to heaviness. Humble yourselves in the sight of the Lord, and He shall lift you up." (4:8-10)*

When we find ourselves without joy because of sin, it is a call to repentance. We can never enjoy the calm delight of the Spirit of God if we are grieving Him by sin left unconfessed and undealt with. We have no right to expect joy when following our own way instead of God's.

But what exactly *is* joy, anyway?

## JOY'S DEFINITION

The word *joy* in Galatians 5:22 is the word *chara*, which has to do with cheerfulness and gladness. The part of the Strong's definition I found the most enlightening was the phrase, "calm delight."

We often think of joy as a frenetic energy, like a small child jumping up and down with excitement they just can't hold in, but that is not what joy is, and I'm glad of that! That kind of excitement is enjoyable for a time, but is intended to fade. We are not built to sustain a frantic happiness for long.

That is why this idea of a calm delight is so helpful to us. For many, joy is elusive because the that which they are seeking is not really joy. Rather than a burst of energetic happiness, joy is meant to stay quietly in the background, to be always there, to be enjoyed continuously. This is Biblical joy, the joy that remains.

Interestingly, this word for joy comes from the same root word as the word grace. Both share an initial root word that means to be happy or well. In fact, that very root word that connects grace and joy could itself be translated as joy or rejoicing. I think this connection between joy and grace is both interesting and informative, because it shows just how much joy is to be a part of the Christian life which is lived, as Titus 2:11 tells us, by the grace of God.

To put it simply, grace is the gift of God that enables us to have abiding joy.

## JOY AND THE GOSPEL

Not only are joy and grace tied together, joy and the gospel are likewise inseparable. When the angels announced the birth of the long-awaited Savior, what did they say?

*"Fear not, for behold, I bring you good tidings of great joy, which shall be to all people." (Luke 2:10)*

We sing songs like "Joy to the World" at Christmas, but as we have already seen, the joy of Christmas is an *abiding* joy. It is the joy of the gospel: Christ came to die in our place, bearing the punishment for our sin and offering the gift of salvation to all people. That is the joy of the gospel.

Acts 8 tells of the first post-resurrection presentation of the gospel in Samaria. Notice its result:

*"Then Philip went down to the city of Samaria, and preached Christ unto them. And the people with one accord gave heed unto those things which Philip spake, hearing and seeing the miracles which he did. For unclean spirits, crying with loud voice, came out of many that were possessed with them: and many*

*taken with palsies, and that were lame, were healed. And there was great joy in that city." (vv.5-8)*

The people *"with one accord"* believed the gospel, and the result was great joy. That brings us to our next point:

## JOY AND FELLOWSHIP

Not only did the truth of the gospel and the salvation it offered bring great joy to the Samaritans, it also brought them into a new kind of fellowship one with another. They were all hearing the gospel and seeing the miracles together, and for those who believed, it was the beginning of a new life in Christ—a new life they shared with their fellow believers.

Of all the "holy men of old" God used to write the Bible, *(2 Peter 1:21)* John was the one who focused the most on fellowship. Both in his gospel and in the three epistles which bear his name, he mentions or describes fellowship quite frequently. In the opening verses of his 1 John, for example, we find the following:

*"That which we have seen and heard declare we unto you, that ye also may have fellowship with us: and truly our fellowship is with the Father and with His Son Jesus Christ. And these things write we unto you, that your joy may be full." (1:3-4)*

Notice first the connection between fellowship and joy. Joy is made full as we learn what John and others had seen and heard of Christ, i.e., the gospel, and as we in turn embrace the fellowship we share with our fellow believers.

This fellowship is rooted in the fact that we have all received the same Spirit. As a preacher I know likes to point out, the Spirit of God in *me* will not fight against the Spirit of God in *you*. If we are walking in the Spirit, there will be a beautiful kind of unity as we exhibit the fruit of the Spirit in our interactions one with another.

So what does joy have to do with our interaction with fellow Christians? Here are a few areas Scripture specifically connects with joy:

## *Giving*

"Moreover, brethren, we do you to wit of the grace of God bestowed on the churches of Macedonia: How that in a great trial of affliction the abundance of their joy and their deep poverty abounded unto the riches of their liberality." (2 Corinthians 8:1-2)

Despite their poverty, the Macedonian Christians had a joy that overflowed in material generosity toward believers in need. When we have a calm delight in the Lord, we will not fuss about giving. Instead, we will trust God's leading and cheerfully, generously give, receiving in return the blessing of being used by God to meet a need.

When we are delighting in God, we will hold loosely to material things, remembering that all has been given by Him, and is given to be used for His glory. We will also look upon our fellow believers with compassion, delighting to be a help where we can.

## *Discipling*

"Moreover I call God for a record upon my soul, that to spare you I came not as yet unto Corinth. Not for that we have dominion over your faith, but are helpers of your joy: for by faith ye stand." (2 Corinthians 1:23-24)

If we look at the context of this passage, we quickly see that Paul is reminding the Corinthian believers of the sincerity of the preaching he and others had presented among them.

Yet as he defends the truth and sincerity of his teaching, he makes this statement about not having dominion over the faith of the Corinthian believers.

It is just a short thought, one which we would easily skim over as we read through the passage, but it speaks volumes to the relationship of believers in a discipleship situation. Instead of lording over these immature Christians, Paul takes the position of helper.

Discipleship means helping another Christian to grow in the Lord. It means coming alongside another, encouraging their obedience to God that they might have the full, abiding joy of the Spirit. To disciple a fellow Christian is to be a helper of their joy.

## *Prayer*

*"I thank my God upon every remembrance of you, Always in every prayer of mine for you all making request with joy, For your fellowship in the gospel from the first day until now; Being confident of this very thing, that He which hath begun a good work in you will perform it until the day of Jesus Christ"* (Philippians 1:3-6)

Part of our interaction with other believers is the fellowship of prayer. When we pray for others, God knits our hearts to them, and when we know that someone has been lifting up prayers on our behalf, it makes them more precious to us. There is a common joy when we pray with other believers and see God work in response.

But sometimes the ministry of prayer, as that of discipleship, hits a season of one-sided effort: when perhaps the one we are discipling or praying for falls away, or refuses to obey the clear commands of Scripture. That is when Paul's prayer for the Philippian Christians can encourage us the most.

He prayed for them, giving thanks for their fellowship in the gospel, *believing* that God would finish the work He had begun in them. When our efforts to disciple or pray for another believer hit a rocky patch, we can still take a calm delight in the fact that God is not done with them yet. The Spirit-born love that never fails motivates us to continue on in prayer and obedience to the Spirit's promptings, persisting with the joy of knowing that God will finish His work.

### Servant-Hearted Ministry

*"For the kingdom of God is not meat and drink; but righteousness, and peace, and joy in the Holy Ghost. For he that in these things serveth Christ is acceptable to God, and approved of men. Let us therefore follow after the things which make for peace, and things wherewith one may edify another."* (Romans 14:17-19)

This passage comes towards the end of a discussion of eating meat offered to idols, but the principle applies to many areas of the Christian life. Essentially, we are called to live lives that are not about ourselves, but about God and others.

Instead of asserting our "right" to do as we please, we should focus on serving God in righteousness, peace, and joy in the Holy Spirit. As we do, we will "follow after," or pursue, those things that will further the peace and edification of our fellow believers.

Please note carefully that this does not mean condoning sin or false doctrine: we are to build up our fellow believers while serving God in *righteousness*. This leaves no room for coddling or excusing sin. Rather, we are to kindly speak the truth in love *(Ephesians 4:15)* in order to build up fellow Christians and help them grow in obedience to God.

This servant-hearted focus on building up others is crucial to the unity of the church; because, left to ourselves, we tend to desire position, power, or popularity. When we serve in the flesh, we become territorial of "our" ministries and lash out at those who we think are threatening that which we see to be our own.

This is just the opposite of Christlike service, however, and works counter to the joy of the Spirit. A self-focused ministry destroys a Christian's joy. The sin of pride which drives such a focus comes between us and God, hindering the Spirit's work of joy and building instead anger, bitterness, fear, and envy.

If anyone had cause for ministry envy it would have been John the Baptist. After all, he had been specially chosen by God before he was born to fulfill a ministry of great importance. He was the forerunner of the Messiah, prophesied long ago to prepare the people for the long-awaited coming of the Savior.

And then, Jesus came. After a relatively short time of public ministry, John's crowds began to diminish, and his followers whom he so faithfully pointed to Christ followed Him instead of John. But instead of being angry, envious, bitter, or afraid, John had joy.

How can this be? Look at what he said:

*"He that hath the bride is the bridegroom: but the friend of the bridegroom, which standeth and heareth him, rejoiceth greatly because of the bridegroom's voice: this my joy therefore is fulfilled. He must increase, but I must decrease." (John 3:29-30)*

Think about a wedding. What is the purpose of the bridesmaids and groomsmen? It is to point attention to the bride and groom, and to help them in whatever way is needful. You wouldn't think much of a bridesmaid or groomsman who tried to upstage the bride and groom, but that is exactly what happens when Christians make their ministry about themselves.

Our job is the same as John's: to point others to Jesus, giving up our "rights" and recognition so that Jesus will be magnified. Like a member of a bridal party in a wedding, the believer's role in the church is to promote the unity of Christ and His bride, which is the church. We are to interact with other believers in humility, seeking to build others up in what Ephesians 4:3 calls *"the unity of the Spirit."*

## JOY AND PERSECUTION

One of the defining differences between the joy of the Spirit and what the world calls joy is its relation to outward circumstances. The world's joy depends on things going well, while the joy of the Spirit not only withstands difficulties and trials, it thrives in them!

In the book of Hebrews, we are told to persevere in the Christian life,

*"Looking unto Jesus, the Author and Finisher of our faith; Who for the joy that was set before Him endured the cross, despising the shame, and is set down at the right hand of the throne of God." (Hebrews 12:2)*

Christ's joy was not found in the *pain* He would suffer, but rather in the *end result* that pain would accomplish. The joy of the result made the difficulties of the process seem like nothing. Christ despised, or viewed as insignificant, the shame of a painful, ignominious death because He was rejoicing that sin's debt would be paid once and for all, and His beloved sinners would be offered full and free forgiveness.

For the Christian, the "end result," so to speak, is heaven. No matter what valleys God leads us through on earth, no matter what pain, sorrow, or trouble, we can keep in our hearts the calm delight of heaven, looking to Jesus as our example.

Paul also gives us a glimpse into joy that transcends trials. In Acts 20, Paul is addressing church leaders from Ephesus as he prepares to leave for Rome. Here is what he told them:

*"And now, behold, I go bound in the Spirit unto Jerusalem, not knowing the things that shall befall me there: Save that the Holy Ghost witnesseth in every city, saying that bonds and afflictions abide me. But none of these things move me, neither count I my life dear unto myself, so that I might finish my course with joy, and the ministry, which I have received of the Lord Jesus, to testify the gospel of the grace of God." (vv. 22-24)*

God had warned Paul that his visit to Rome would not be pleasant, and yet that did not worry him. His focus was not on the pain he would endure, but on the joy of finishing well, of completing the work God had called him to do.

Much earlier, in Acts 13, Paul and Barnabas are thrown out of a city where they had been peaceably preaching the gospel. They had poured much effort into this city, and had been faithful to witness to both Jews and Gentiles, but found themselves expelled from the city. What did they do?

*"But they shook off the dust of their feet against them, and came unto Iconium. And the disciples were filled with joy and with the Holy Ghost." (vv.51-52)*

Instead of fussing at God, or whining about their misfortunes to each other, the two men got back to work, leaving the city and its inhabitants to God. When they focused on the task at hand, they were filled with joy and the Holy Spirit. That is grace in action. As we get our focus off those who have mistreated us and onto our next step of obedience to God, the Holy Spirit will fill us with a calm delight. We are not meant to bear the burden of others' actions: God is the judge, and we can safely leave with Him any persecutors we may encounter.

Contrary to what we would naturally think, Jesus said that true persecution is actually a *cause* for rejoicing.

*"Blessed are ye, when men shall hate you, and when they shall separate you from their company, and shall reproach you, and cast out your name as evil, for the Son of Man's sake. Rejoice ye in that day, and leap for joy: for behold, your reward is great in heaven: for in the like manner did their fathers unto the prophets." (Luke 6:22-23)*

This is why the disciples in Acts 5 rejoiced when threatened and beaten by the Jewish leaders.

*"And they departed from the presence of the council, rejoicing that they were counted worthy to suffer shame for His name" (v. 41)*

Instead of discouraging the disciples, the council's persecution *encouraged* them to be bold for Christ! When we face persecution for the sake of Christ, we likewise can be encouraged, for *"all that will live godly in Christ Jesus shall suffer persecution." (2 Timothy 3:12)*

## JOY AND TRIALS

Not all difficulties we face in life will be due to persecution. What significance does joy have when we are facing the other hard things of life? James 1 tells us,

*"My brethren, count it all joy when ye fall into divers temptations; Knowing this, that the trying of your faith worketh patience."(vv.2-3)*

God never allows anything into our lives which He does not intend to use for our good. When we come face to face with a trial, we can do so with a calm delight that trusts that God is going to do something good through it. This joy does not necessarily lessen the pain or sorrow of the trial, but it does give us hope and peace as we go through it, knowing God is right there with us.

1 Peter also gives us some perspective on trials and joy:

*"That the trial of your faith, being much more precious than of gold that perisheth, though it be tried with fire, might be found unto praise and honour and glory at the appearing of Jesus Christ: Whom having not seen, ye love; in Whom, though now ye see Him not, yet believing, ye rejoice with joy unspeakable and full of glory" (1:7-8)*

Our joy in trials is not that we *have* a trial, but that *through it*, God is building our faith. Though we cannot see Christ, we nevertheless find joy "unspeakable and full of glory" in the truth that He *is* and that He will appear again. We can rejoice in the certainty of Christ's return and our eternity to come in the presence of God, no matter what trial we face here on earth.

If our eyes are fixed on Christ, nothing can dim our true joy. Our calm delight in all that God is and has promised will transcend all earthly sorrows and difficulties.

# 4

# Peace

*"But the fruit of the Spirit is love, joy, peace, longsuffering, gentleness, goodness, faith, Meekness, temperance: against such there is no law."*
*Galatians 5:22-23*

Like love and joy, peace is closely intertwined with the other qualities of the fruit of the Spirit. The Greek word used here for *peace* means quietness, rest, or unity. It is referred to in the New Testament many times and is a key component of both the greetings and closings of many New Testament books.

In the Old Testament, the Hebrew equivalent is the word *Shalom* which means to be safe, well, or happy, and could also be translated as friendly, or refer to one's welfare in terms of health and peace.

*Shalom* is a common greeting among Jews, and hence it is not surprising to see it used so commonly as a greeting between Christians in the early church. Jesus Himself used the word *peace* as a greeting to His disciples throughout the gospels.

Peace is such a common word throughout the New Testament, it can be difficult to know where to begin studying it out, but as with anything, it is usually best to begin at the beginning.

## PEACE WITH GOD

When the angels appeared before the shepherds after the announcement of the newborn Savior, they proclaimed,

*"Glory to God in the highest, and on earth peace, good will toward men."* (Luke 2:14)

Looking around at our world today, you might wonder where that "peace on earth" went! Yet, Christ came not to establish an earthly peace between nations, but rather a heavenly peace on earth in the hearts of His followers. Jesus said,

*"These things I have spoken unto you, that in Me ye might have peace. In the world ye shall have tribulation: but be of good cheer; I have overcome the world." (John 16:33)*

Jesus offers us peace that—like joy—transcends earthly circumstances. But in order to enjoy this peace, we first have to be reconciled to God: to have peace *with* God. Romans 5:1-2 says,

*"Therefore being justified by faith, we have peace with God through our Lord Jesus Christ; By whom also we have access by faith into this grace wherein we stand, and rejoice in hope of the glory of God."*

This is a packed verse, but notice how we *get* peace with God: we are justified by faith, through Christ. We all need to be justified, because as Romans 3:23 says,

*"all have sinned and come short of the glory of God."*

Christ's sacrifice paid the penalty for all our sin, giving each individual the opportunity to be made right with God. Ephesians 2 puts it this way:

*"But now in Christ Jesus ye who sometimes were far off are made nigh by the blood of Christ. For He is our peace, who hath made both one, and hath broken down the middle wall of partition between us" (vv.13-14)*

Christ's payment of our penalty satisfied the perfect justice of God, while at the same time showing His mercy to us. Once we have placed our faith in Christ, trusting His sacrifice alone to justify us in the sight of God, we are no longer separated from God. Our sin is covered by the blood of Jesus, and we can enter into a real relationship with God. We are no longer enemies. We are family. Galatians 4 explains,

*"But when the fulness of the time was come, God sent forth His Son, made of a woman, made under the law, To redeem them that were under the law, that we might receive the adoption of sons. And because ye are sons, God hath sent forth the Spirit of His Son into your hearts, crying, Abba, Father. Wherefore thou art no more a servant, but a son; and if a son, then an heir of God through Christ." (vv.4-7)*

One aspect of our adoption is the sending of the Holy Spirit. Peace comes from the Holy Spirit indwelling our hearts, helping us to be rightly related to God.

## THE GOD OF PEACE

Throughout the New Testament, God is referred to as *the God of peace*. What does the God of peace do? There are two areas specifically connected in Scripture to God being the God of peace: sanctification and victory:

## Sanctification

Sanctification is the process by which God makes us more and more like Himself. It is the purging of sin and strengthening of our faith. The word *sanctify* means to make holy

> *"And the very God of peace sanctify you wholly; and I pray God your whole spirit and soul and body be preserved blameless unto the coming of our Lord Jesus Christ. Faithful is He that calleth you, Who also will do it." (1 Thessalonians 5:23-24)*

Notice here how much God sanctifies us: *wholly*. The mention of spirit, soul, and body also adds to the idea of completeness. Sanctification is to affect every part of us: our minds, our souls, and our physical bodies.

That seems like a hard standard to meet, but that is why I included that next verse: *"Faithful is He that calleth you, Who also will do it."* You see, we are not expected to be holy in our own power. It is the power of God that does the work: we just have to decide to let Him do it.

Hebrews 13:20-21 reminds us how powerful the God of peace is:

> *"Now the God of peace, that brought again from the dead our Lord Jesus, that great shepherd of the sheep, through the blood of the everlasting covenant, Make you perfect in every good work to do His will, working in you that which is wellpleasing in His sight, through Jesus Christ; to Whom be glory for ever and ever. Amen."*

The same God who raised Jesus from the dead is the God who works in us, so that we can do His will by His own power.

That word *"perfect"* is a word that means to repair or restore, to thoroughly complete. The process of sanctification is the restoration of the holiness God always intended for us. It is the repairing of the brokenness caused by our sin. In this way, sanctification is about restoring peace.

Holiness and peace are connected often in Scripture: 2 Timothy, for example, says:

*"Flee also youthful lusts: but follow righteousness, faith, charity, peace, with them that call on the Lord out of a pure heart." (2:22)*

And 1 Peter 3:10-11 declares,

*"For he that will love life, and see good days, let him refrain his tongue from evil, and his lips that they speak no guile: Let him eschew evil, and do good; let him seek peace, and ensue it."*

The word *"ensue"* means to follow after, to press forward in pursuit as if to persecute. We are to pursue peace, to doggedly keep after it, determined not to rest without it. We should seek God's peace with a sense of urgency.

### Victory

*"And the God of peace shall bruise Satan under your feet shortly. The grace of our Lord Jesus Christ be with you. Amen." (Romans 16:20)*

In modern America, many of us live far removed from the idea of war. Victory to us is the idea of winning, accomplishing a feat, or overcoming an obstacle. But for Christians in the age of Rome (and in many countries of the world even today) peace often primarily meant freedom from violence.

In a spiritual sense, the peace of God is not just about relationship, it is also about victory over the sin that attacks that relationship. We are told,

*"Be sober, be vigilant; because your adversary the devil, as a roaring lion, walketh about, seeking whom he may devour." (1 Peter 5:8)*

Satan's goal is the opposite of God's. We know that God desires His people to be sanctified, to grow in holiness. Satan wants not only to prevent our growth, but also to undo any progress we have made. That is why 1 Corinthians 10:12 says,

*"Wherefore let him that thinketh he standeth take heed lest he fall."*

Sanctification is more than just overcoming obstacles: it is a fight against a real and literal foe who actively seeks to destroy us in any way he can. Yet the battle is not in our own strength, but in God's. That's why it is *God* who will crush Satan under our feet.

Because Satan's fight is ultimately against God, Satan is destined to lose. In fact, his final fate is detailed already in Revelation 20:10. He cannot win. We ought to be vigilant of his attacks, but we need not be afraid of him, for we belong to God. It is God's power that will protect and strengthen us in our fight.

## PEACE OF MIND

When we use the phrase "peace of mind," we often mean it to encompass both mind and emotions. The peace of God is a perfect peace that fills every part of us, quieting both the restless mind and the anxious heart.

I am naturally prone to worry, and one of my friends frequently has occasion to remind me of Philippians 4:6-7, which says,

*"Be careful for nothing; but in every thing by prayer and supplication with thanksgiving let your requests be made known unto God. And the peace of*

God, which passeth understanding, shall keep your hearts and minds through Christ Jesus." (Philippians 4:6-7)*

I don't know about you, but I like to figure things out. I over-analyze and spend countless hours imagining out possibilities and scenarios, but there are so many things in life I just can't understand. That is why it is important to remember that the peace of God *"passeth understanding."*

It doesn't matter if we can figure things out because God is omniscient and sovereign. We can rest quietly in the knowledge that whatever is happening, whatever we don't understand, God knows, and is in control. Nothing ever perplexes Him or takes Him by surprise.

It is easy to underestimate the importance of our thoughts, but Romans 8:6 says,

*"For to be carnally minded is death; but to be spiritually minded is life and peace."*

That phrase, *"carnally minded,"* means to have thinking that is in line with our naturally sinful flesh. It is to think as if we have never been made alive in Christ, as if we were still *"dead in trespasses and sins."* (Ephesians 2:1)

Peace comes as we surrender our own desire to figure things out on our own and decide to trust God instead. Only then will the peace of God keep, or protect, both our hearts and minds. We find this same truth in Isaiah 26:3:

*"Thou wilt keep him in perfect peace, whose mind is stayed on Thee: because he trusteth in Thee."*

In order to have that perfect peace of heart, we must first "stay," or steady, our minds on the Lord. This is where the wrestling against our flesh often begins. But our sinful thoughts and emotions *can* be controlled. 2 Corinthians 10:4-5 says,

> *"For the weapons of our warfare are not carnal, but mighty through God to the pulling down of strong holds;) Casting down imaginations, and every high thing that exalteth itself against the knowledge of God, and bringing into captivity every thought to the obedience of Christ"*

The battle against sin often begins in the mind, and it takes the power of God to win it. It takes effort to decide to obey and not to let our minds dwell on ungodly thoughts. I think that is why God chose to couch the verse above in military terms, taking thoughts captive, bringing them back in line with obedience to Christ. As with anything else, we cannot have victory over our thoughts without the power of the Holy Spirit.

Our thoughts show what we really believe about God. For example, when we worry, we are *thinking* as if God isn't good, powerful, or in control. To worry is to display a lack of faith that God is who He has said He is, or that He will do what He has promised. That is why Philippians 4:6 tells us to be *"careful for nothing."*

But how are we to do that? The verse goes on to tell us that the antidote to worry is prayer. As we pray, bringing our requests to God, our hearts and minds are brought into line with the Holy Spirit, and we trade our worries for peace.

And notice *how* we are supposed to bring our requests to God:

> *"in every thing by prayer and supplication with thanksgiving let your requests be made known unto God"* (Philippians 4:6)

The giving of thanks is a crucial part of having a heart and mind filled with the peace of God. Colossians 3:15 says,

*"And let the peace of God rule in your hearts, to the which also ye are called in one body; and be ye thankful."*

When the peace of God rules in our hearts, we will have an attitude of thankfulness. Discontent and ingratitude are contrary to the peace of God. In fact, *"unthankful"* is one of the terms used to describe the wickedness of the people in the last days, and is closely followed by the word *"unholy"*. (2 Timothy 3:2)

The peace of God means bringing our thoughts under the control of the Holy Spirit, bringing our sorrows and problems to God instead of keeping them to ourselves, and also allowing the Holy Spirit to cultivate in us a heart of gratefulness to God.

## PEACE WITH OTHERS

The Holy Spirit's primary work is *inside* the Christian, in the heart and mind, but as faith without works is dead, *(James 2:20)* so internal sanctification without a change in outward attitudes and actions is not true sanctification. A changed heart will always lead to changed actions.

The emphasis, of course, is on the heart, but the actions are an important outworking of what is going on in the heart. This is why the characteristics of the fruit of the Spirit are linked with our interactions with others. Peace is no exception.

Remember the admonition of Romans 14:17-19 which we looked at in our study of joy? Notice again what it says we should follow after, or pursue.

*"For the kingdom of God is not meat and drink; but righteousness, and peace, and joy in the Holy Ghost. For he that in these things serveth Christ is*

*acceptable to God, and approved of men. Let us therefore follow after the things which make for peace, and things wherewith one may edify another."*

When the peace of God rules our hearts and minds, we will look to help others have that peace as well. This could mean sharing the truth of the gospel to point a lost one to peace with God, or it could mean helping another believer grow in their own submission to the Holy Spirit so that they can enjoy the peace of God as well. Whatever the practical steps the Holy Spirit leads us to take, the peace of God will lead us to do what we can to help others have the same peace. When we are filled with the peace of God, we will desire to help others find God's peace for themselves.

Another outworking of God's work of peace within us is peace between ourselves and others:

*"I therefore, the prisoner of the Lord, beseech you that ye walk worthy of the vocation wherewith ye are called, With all lowliness and meekness, with longsuffering, forbearing one another in love; endeavoring to keep the unity of the Spirit in the bond of peace." (Ephesians 4:1-3)*

We'll come back to this verse again later on when we study longsuffering, but notice what this humble meek behavior is to accomplish: the keeping of the unity of the Spirit in the bond of peace. When the Holy Spirit is keeping our hearts and minds in peace, we will not have friction with other Christians who are also walking in obedience to the Holy Spirit.

This unity of the Spirit is destroyed easily, however, by the sin of pride. Proverbs 13:10 says,

*"Only by pride cometh contention: but with the well advised is wisdom."*

Our flesh hates to forbear, to show longsuffering and to respond to another's pride with meekness, but that is exactly how the Holy Spirit will lead us to respond. James 3 illustrates this well:

> "Who is a wise man and endued with knowledge among you? Let him shew out of a good conversation his works with meekness of wisdom. But if ye have bitter envying and strife in your hearts, glory not, and lie not against the truth. This wisdom descendeth not from above, but is earthly, sensual, devilish. For where envying and strife is, there is confusion and every evil work. But the wisdom that is from above is first pure, then peaceable, gentle, and easy to be intreated, full of mercy and good fruits, without partiality, and without hypocrisy. And the fruit of righteousness is sown in peace of them that make peace." (vv.13-18)

Our sinful flesh regards humility, forbearance, and meekness as proof of weakness, when in fact it takes more strength than we possess to respond properly to even the well-meaning around us. Notice that the wisdom of God is *peaceable*. When we are walking in accordance with the Spirit of God, His peace in our hearts and minds will keep envying, strife, and confusion out, leading us to be peaceable towards others instead.

This does not guarantee that we will always live friction-free lives with those around us. Even the most Spirit-led Christians in our lives are still sinners saved by grace, and so are we. In addition to this, the world hates true peace, because it comes from the holy God who sees their sin as it really is. I think this is why Romans 12:18 admonishes us,

> "If it be possible, as much as lieth in you, live peaceably with all men."

It may not always be possible to keep peace with others, particularly if they have not received Christ as their Savior. It is, however, our responsibility to make sure that any friction between us and others is not due to sinful actions or attitudes on our part.

## PEACE ALWAYS

Just as Jesus said that His joy was to remain, peace is likewise to be an ever-present quality of the Spirit-led life. 2 Thessalonians 3:16 says,

> "Now the Lord of peace Himself give you peace always by all means. The Lord be with you all."

We are to have peace *always*. Not just when we are sitting in the early morning quiet with our cup of coffee and our Bible, not just when things are going well, not just when we feel like everything is right with the world: but *always*.

No matter what is going on around us, we have access to the peace of God at all times, if we will only surrender our hearts and minds to the Holy Spirit's control. Placing our minds, wills, and emotions in the care of the Holy Spirit, not allowing any ungodly thought to roam free, committing all to the care of the God who cares for us: that is how we live a life of peace.

> *"Now the God of hope fill you with all joy and peace in believing, that ye may abound in hope, through the power of the Holy Ghost."*
> *Romans 15:13*

# 5

# Longsuffering

*"But the fruit of the Spirit is love, joy, peace, longsuffering, gentleness, goodness, faith, Meekness, temperance: against such there is no law."*
*Galatians 5:22-23*

None of us like to suffer, particularly when the suffering is of a long duration. Perhaps that is why the word longsuffering has so little appeal. Yet longsuffering is a crucial characteristic of the fruit of the Spirit. It is one way love is demonstrated in our interactions with others, for *"Charity suffereth long, and is kind." (1 Corinthians 13:4)*

Longsuffering is the very patience of God shown to others through the conduit of His people.

The word most commonly translated as *longsuffering* in the New Testament, including Galatians 5:22, means longsuffering, forbearance, or fortitude. The word *longsuffering*, as the Bible uses it, has the idea of bearing with others graciously for however long is needful, losing neither patience nor temper.

Like the other characteristics of the fruit of the Spirit, longsuffering is an attribute best displayed by God Himself.

## OUR LONGSUFFERING GOD

In Exodus 34, Moses stood on Mount Sinai, waiting. If you are familiar with the account, you know that Moses had asked to see God, who had told Moses that he could not see the face of God, but that Moses would see a part of God's glory as He passed by. Moses followed God's instructions, and God showed up, just as He had promised. Notice what God says here about Himself:

*"And the Lord descended in the cloud, and stood with him there, and proclaimed the name of the Lord. And the Lord passed by before him, and proclaimed, The Lord, The Lord God, merciful and gracious, longsuffering, and abundant in goodness and truth, Keeping mercy for thousands, forgiving iniquity and transgression and sin, and that will by no means clear the guilty; visiting the iniquity of the fathers upon the children, and upon the children's children, unto the third and to the fourth generation." (Exodus 34:5-7)*

This passage shows us that God Himself views His longsuffering as a foundational part of who He is. Also, notice the interplay between His justice and His longsuffering. He does not clear the guilty, but neither does He pour out His wrath upon them prematurely. This longsuffering towards unforgiven sinners is seen in 2 Peter 3:9, which says,

*"The Lord is not slack concerning His promise, as some men count slackness; but is longsuffering to us-ward, not willing that any should perish, but that all should come to repentance."*

The context of this verse is a passage dealing with the certainty of Christ's return, and His mercy in waiting for the proper moment. Just as He did with Israel all those years before the Babylonian captivity,

God is displaying His longsuffering towards the sinful human race by giving each individual time to respond to His call to repent and believe.

God's longsuffering is not to be taken for granted, however. God is longsuffering, but not unjustly so. Just as God brought judgment upon Israel at the proper time, there will be a time of judgment for each unbeliever. Note these verses from the book of Romans:

*"And thinkest thou this, O man, that judgest them which do such things, and doest the same, that thou shalt escape the judgement of God? Or despisest thou the riches of His goodness and forbearance and longsuffering; not knowing that the goodness of God leadeth thee to repentance?" (Romans 2:3-4)*

To presume upon God's longsuffering is to reject His goodness and ignore His justice. For the Christian, presuming upon God's longsuffering means ignoring or rejecting the clear commands of Scripture in the assumption that God will overlook it "this time". Not only is this presumption outright sin, it also results in grieving the Holy Spirit (Ephesians 4:30.)

The longsuffering of God is a glorious thing, for which we ought to find ourselves ever more grateful each day, and yet we often get annoyed at God's longsuffering towards others who we feel deserve His swift and full judgment.

We, like the unjust steward in Matthew 18, having been extended the longsuffering of our good Master, which we did not deserve, then turn to our fellow sinners and demand immediate retribution for their sins. If God suffered long with you and me, how dare we begrudge any other sinner of the longsuffering God bestows upon them!

## EXAMPLES OF LONGSUFFERING

Throughout Scripture, we see those whom God highlights displaying longsuffering towards others. Think of Joseph serving well in prison, though he had done nothing wrong. Think of Moses pleading with God for the people over and over again, though it was *Moses* at whom the people's anger and mistrust were directed. Or consider David, refusing to harm Saul, though Saul clearly intended to kill David.

The New Testament also has examples of longsuffering, the best example of all being the Lord Jesus:

*"For even hereunto were ye called: because Christ also suffered for us, leaving us an example, that ye should follow His steps: Who did no sin, neither was guile found in His mouth: Who, when He was reviled, reviled not again; when He suffered, He threatened not; but committed Himself to Him that judgeth righteously."* (1 Peter 2:21-23)

We can sometimes feel as if the example of Christ is too perfect to strive for: after all, He *is* God. Of course He didn't sin! This reaction to Christ's example is completely natural, but wholly wrong. The perfection of Christ does not negate His example to us any more than a teacher's deep knowledge of a subject negates a student's ability to learn from it. We need Christ's example to show us how God wants us to respond to others.

This perfect example of Christ is given, not to discourage us, but rather to *encourage* us. Hebrews 12 says,

*"Wherefore seeing we also are compassed about with so great a cloud of witnesses, let us lay aside every weight, and the sin which doth so easily beset us, and let us run with patience the race that is set before us, Looking unto Jesus the Author and Finisher of our faith; Who for the joy that was set before Him endured the cross, despising the shame, and is set down at the right hand of the throne of God. For consider Him that endured such contradiction of sinners against Himself, lest ye be wearied and faint in your minds. Ye have not yet resisted unto blood, striving against sin."* (vv.1-4)

Whatever seasons of longsuffering God calls us to walk through, we can look to Christ's example and be encouraged that He has already victoriously walked a far more difficult path of longsuffering, and that He is the one who offers us *His* power to walk our own path in victory.

There are other examples given to us in the New Testament as well, such as Stephen, who preached Christ to the Jewish religious leaders and remained calm and steadfast even as he was led outside the city and stoned to death. And then there's Paul, who faced almost constant persecution, yet was able to say to Timothy, who had traveled with him,

*"But thou hast fully known my doctrine, manner of life, purpose, faith, longsuffering, charity, patience, Persecutions, afflictions, which came unto me at Antioch, at Iconium, at Lystra; what persecutions I endured: but out of them all the Lord delivered me." (2 Timothy 3:10-11)*

Those who had known Paul personally had seen him respond toward others with longsuffering. They knew his patience and forbearance because they had witnessed it themselves. A challenging thought for you and me is, do those closest to us know *our* longsuffering firsthand?

James 5:10-11 points us to more examples of longsuffering:

*"Take, my brethren, the prophets, who have spoken in the name of the Lord, for an example of suffering affliction, and of patience. Behold, we count them happy which endure. Ye have heard of the patience of Job, and have seen the end of the Lord; that the Lord is very pitiful, and of tender mercy."*

Imagine the longsuffering of prophets like Hosea, Isaiah, Jeremiah, and so many others, who faithfully preached God's Word to a rebellious people. Part of their role as prophets was to show forth the longsuffering of God, as well as the reality of His coming judgment.

The book of Hebrews also points us to human examples of longsuffering:

*"And we desire that every one of you do show the same diligence to the full assurance of hope unto the end: That ye be not slothful, but followers of them who through faith and patience inherit the promises. For when God made promise to Abraham, because He could swear by no greater, He sware by Himself, Saying, Surely blessing I will bless thee, and multiplying I will multiply thee. And so, after he had patiently endured, he obtained the promise." (6:11-15)*

The longsuffering of those gone before encourages us not to be lazy in our Christian walk, but rather to go on diligently heeding the promptings of the Spirit, knowing that God will be just as faithful to us as He was to them. The same God who kept His covenant with Abraham will keep the promises made to us throughout Scripture. This gives us hope, which Hebrews 6:19 later describes so beautifully:

*"Which hope we have as an anchor of the soul, both sure and stedfast."*

## OUR LONGSUFFERING

This is where it gets difficult. The examples of God's longsuffering throughout Scripture and the pictures of the victorious longsuffering of the saints of old will do nothing for us unless we *act* upon their example. There are many commands in the New Testament for believers to live out Holy-Spirit empowered longsuffering:

### *Forgiveness*

*"Put on therefore, as the elect of God, holy and beloved, bowels of mercies, kindness, humbleness of mind, meekness, longsuffering;Forbearing one another, and forgiving one another, if any man have a quarrel against any: even as Christ forgave you, so also do ye." (Colossians 3:12-13)*

Longsuffering means being willing not just to forbear, but also to forgive. There is no room in a Spirit-filled heart for bitterness or unforgiveness. Christ forgave you all your sins against Him, and calls you to do likewise.

A refusal to bear grudges is a notable quality in our current world that clamors for their "rights" and demands retribution for any wrongs done them. Yet this is exactly what Christ did—remember His cry from the cross of,

*"Father, forgive them, for they know not what they do." (Luke 23:34)*

The very soldiers who had driven nails into His hands and feet stood at the foot of the cross and heard Him forgive them. The religious leaders who had plotted, schemed, and lied to get Him crucified also heard that plea for forgiveness on their behalf.

Forgiveness when grievously wronged was likewise common among early believers. Stephen, for example, cried out loudly while being stoned to death:

*"Lord, lay not this sin to their charge." (Acts 7:60)*

Notice that these pleas for God's forgiveness of tormenters were not just internal: each was loudly proclaimed for all to hear. When we extend forgiveness to someone, it is good and right to make sure they *know* it. You never know when there is a Saul standing by who will have need of the knowledge of your forgiveness for his wrongdoing when he has repented later on.

The Christians of the early church and those down through the centuries who have faced persecution have typically been quick to forgive their persecutors, even in the midst of torture, and often unto death. Yet we who live in peaceful lands, free from the threat of violence, are typically quick to take up an offense and slow to offer forgiveness. May it not take an outbreak of persecution to teach us to forgive others as quickly, freely, and fully, as Christ has forgiven us!

Earlier in the book of Colossians, Paul told the Christians at Colossae that He prayed for them,

*"That ye might walk worthy of the Lord unto all pleasing, being fruitful in every good work, and increasing in the knowledge of God; Strengthened with all might, according to His glorious power, unto all patience and longsuffering with joyfulness." (1:10-11)*

Notice that when we are strengthened with His might, and according to His power, the result is not only patience and joy as we have already discussed, but also longsuffering. Just like every other characteristic of the fruit of the Spirit, longsuffering takes the power of God empowering us to obey.

## *Fellowship*

Our Spirit-empowered longsuffering is also crucial to the health of the local church:

*"I therefore, the prisoner of the Lord, beseech you that ye walk worthy of the vocation wherewith ye are called, With all lowliness and meekness, with longsuffering, forbearing one another in love; Endeavoring to keep the unity of the Spirit in the bond of peace." (Ephesians 4:1-3)*

When Christians fail to demonstrate longsuffering towards one another, it destroys the unity of the Spirit. Lowliness, meekness, longsuffering, and forbearance are all results of walking in the Spirit. When we are impatient, critical, prideful, or envious of one another, we are not walking in the Spirit, but in the flesh. Galatians 5:17 points out that the flesh and the Spirit are *"contrary one to the other,"* thus a Christian walking in the flesh will not get along well with a Christian who is walking in the Spirit. As we have noted in a previous chapter, Proverbs 13:10 tells us that,

*"Only by pride cometh contention: but with the well advised is wisdom."*

When we are experiencing friction between ourselves and another believer, it is our duty to first make sure that we ourselves are walking in the Spirit, and then to humbly extend to our brother or sister in Christ the loving longsuffering God has called us to. The church will experience its greatest unity when its members are choosing to yield to the Holy Spirit in their interactions one with another.

The church is made up of redeemed sinners. One day, we will all be in heaven in new sinless bodies, and in perfect unity one with another. But this side of heaven, though redeemed, we each still battle a very real, very strong sin nature. That is why longsuffering and its companions, forbearance and forgiveness, are so crucial to the health of the church.

The saved, however, are not the only ones to whom the Christian is called to show longsuffering:

*"Now we exhort you, brethren, warn them that are unruly, comfort the feebleminded, support the weak, be patient toward all men."* (1 Thessalonians 5:14)

I often find myself making excuses for why I "can't" be longsuffering towards those I find most irritating or exasperating, but it is God who has called me to longsuffering, and with the Holy Spirit to empower my obedience, there is really no excuse. The word *patient* in the verse above is the same Greek word translated *longsuffering* in Galatians 5:22. Longsuffering is to be shown to *all*.

## *Doctrine*

Longsuffering also puts our doctrine on display:

*"Preach the Word; be instant in season, out of season; reprove, rebuke, exhort with all longsuffering and doctrine." (2 Timothy 4:2)*

Notice how this verse links longsuffering with doctrine. Every Christian has the responsibility to share the gospel with the lost and to help their fellow believers grow in their understanding of the Bible. This Biblical teaching must be accompanied by longsuffering in order to be effective.

Witnessing and discipleship are not just the spewing of Bible truths at a specific target: both are built upon compassion. It is the love of God that motivates us to share the gospel *(2 Corinthians 5:14)* and it is likewise the love of God that leads us to do the work of exhorting, warning, comforting, and supporting spoken of in 1 Thessalonians 5:14.

Truth without compassion is still truth, but it is unlikely to reach the heart. Doctrine proclaimed with impatience will not incline the hearer to submit to its truth. However, the dedicated commitment displayed by longsuffering will have a lasting impact on those to whom we are communicating truth. The old adage that people will only care how much we know when they know how much we care is perhaps a bit overused, but is nevertheless true.

Longsuffering is not just for witnessing and discipleship, however. Look at what we are to be *patient*, (the same word as longsuffering) for in James 5:7-8:

*"Be patient therefore, brethren, unto the coming of the Lord. Behold, the husbandman waiteth for the precious fruit of the earth, and hath long patience for it, until he receive the early and latter rain. Be ye also patient; stablish your hearts: for the coming of the Lord draweth nigh."*

The return of Christ can seem a long way off as we go about our daily lives in this wicked world. Yet, we do not know when Christ will come; and throughout the New Testament, we are reminded to live in the expectancy of Christ's imminent return.

Waiting can be hard, but a key part of our lives on this earth is the patient anticipation of the return of Christ. The illustration given us in this verse is that of a farmer planting a seed and waiting for it with *"long patience."* Just as the farmer cannot do anything to hasten the harvest day, so we cannot make Christ's return come any faster. We must endure with long patience while watching, waiting, and working.

And we must wait, watch, and work not only *without* complaint, but *with* joy. After all, the fruit of the Spirit is love, joy, peace *and* longsuffering. To separate longsuffering from the other qualities of the fruit of the Spirit is to turn it into a heavy, cheerless thing.

The longsuffering of the Holy Spirit waits with hope, for love *"hopeth all things."* (1 Corinthians 13:7) It waits in joy, delighting in the beauty of the perfect timing of our omniscient God. It waits in peace, trusting that God is in control and will one day make all things new. (Revelation 21:5)

Through the Holy Spirit, we can pour into others the truth of Scripture with genuine compassion and committed love. We can bear with others graciously, with a heart quick to forgive and overlook offenses. We can lavish upon others the longsuffering which God has so generously lavished on us. And we can wait with patience for God's timing.

*"As for God, His way is perfect"*
(Psalm 18:30a)

# 6

# Gentleness

*"But the fruit of the Spirit is love, joy, peace, longsuffering, gentleness, goodness, faith, Meekness, temperance: against such there is no law."*
*Galatians 5:22-23*

When I looked up the word *gentleness* in my Strong's concordance, I found that this particular word is only translated as gentleness here in Galatians 5:22. Elsewhere in the New Testament it is translated as *kindness, graciousness,* and once (in Matthew 11:30) *easy.* Its definition also includes moral excellence in character or demeanor.

The gentleness of the Holy Spirit encompasses all these things: from moral excellence to gentleness and kindness, to "easy" treatment of others, not harsh or exacting. It is what God Himself put on display when He chose to offer salvation to sinners who were unworthy, yet beloved by God.

## THE GENTLENESS OF GOD

*"But God, who is rich in mercy, for His great love wherewith He loved us, Even when we were dead in sins, hath quickened us together with Christ, (by*

grace ye are saved;) And hath raised us up together, and made us sit together in heavenly places in Christ Jesus: That in the ages to come He might shew the exceeding riches of His grace in His kindness toward us through Christ Jesus." (Ephesians 2:4-7)

God is glorified by the display of His gentle kindness towards mankind. It was kindness to the utterly undeserving that prompted Christ's sacrifice on the cross. It was moral excellence of the highest degree that satisfied justice at the expense of selfless sacrifice on the part of the Judge Himself. It was gentleness that responded in mercy and love to those dead in sins, deserving of punishment in hell forever. In Matthew 11:28-30, Jesus calls out,

*"Come unto Me, all ye that labour and are heavy laden, and I will give you rest. Take My yoke upon you, and learn of Me; for I am meek and lowly in heart: and ye shall find rest unto your souls. For My yoke is easy, and My burden is light."*

In our day, we tend to define *easy* as requiring little or no effort, but this word is used in the older sense of the word: to ease a pain or burden, or to put someone at ease. Christ bore the full weight of our sin, that He might offer to us His "easy" burden in exchange.

This is the gentleness of the Good Shepherd, who lays down His life for His sheep *(John 10:11)*. It is the gentleness of the Lord that saves and keeps us; and it is also His gentleness that motivates us to live Christlike lives, treating others with the same gentleness God has demonstrated towards us. In Luke 6:35, Jesus tells us,

*"But love ye your enemies, and do good, and lend, hoping for nothing again; and your reward shall be great, and ye shall be the children of the Highest: for He is kind unto the unthankful and to the evil."*

Here we see not only the kindness (same word as gentleness) of

God, but also longsuffering, humbly doing right, whether or not we see a return—even expecting no return for our kindnesses. That is the gentleness of God in action.

## A Taste for the Word

Not only is the gentleness of God to motivate us to the same kind of unselfish kindness He has shown us, it is also to cause us to thirst after God. 1 Peter 2:1-3 says,

*"Wherefore, laying aside all malice, and all guile, and hypocrisies, and envies, and all evil speakings, As newborn babes, desire the sincere milk of the Word, that ye may grow thereby: If so be ye have tasted that the Lord is gracious."*

The word translated *taste* in this verse has the idea of experiencing. The more we experience God's graciousness, the more motivated we will be to learn and obey and invite others to *"taste and see that the Lord is good." (Psalm 34:8)* We will desire to feed on God's Word, to grow in our relationship with Him and our knowledge of Him.

We will love the Word of God more and more because of the gracious God revealed within its pages. We will delight to obey the One who has shown such gentle kindness to us; and in our obedience, find God more gracious still. It is a blessed cycle rooted in the truth that God is gracious to His children.

Titus 3 also describes the motivating power of God's gentleness (translated here as *kindness*.)

*"Put them in mind to be subject to principalities and powers, to obey magistrates, to be ready to every good work, To speak evil of no man, to be no brawlers, but gentle, shewing all meekness to all men. For we ourselves also were sometimes foolish, disobedient, deceived, serving divers lusts and*

*pleasures, living in malice and envy, hateful, and hating one another. But after that the kindness and love of God our Saviour toward man appeared, Not by works of righteousness which we have done, but according to His mercy He saved us, by the washing of regeneration, and renewing of the Holy Ghost; Which He shed on us abundantly through Jesus Christ our Saviour; That being justified by His grace, we should be made heirs according to the hope of eternal life." (vv.1-7)*

This is a lengthy passage, but it shows how the gentleness of God towards us *"while we were yet sinners" (Romans 5:8)* reminds us to show the same kind of selfless gentleness toward others.

### *That the Ministry be Not Blamed*

The call to imitate Christ is all-encompassing, reaching every area of life, and every situation we face. Whatever others may do, you and I are called to respond—as Christ would—in gentleness.

The apostle Paul is a good example of this all-encompassing call. Though recognizing himself as a sinner, even the "chief" of sinners *(1 Timothy 1:15)*, he still strove to live in obedience to the Holy Spirit, to the point of being able to tell the believers in Corinth as well as Philippi to follow his example as he followed the example of Christ. *(1 Corinthians 4:16; 11:1; Philippians 3:17)*

I wonder, can others be led to greater Christlikeness by following our example? It is a convicting thought, but as Christians, Jesus tells us to

*"Let your light so shine before men, that they may see your good works, and glorify your Father which is in heaven." (Matthew 5:16)*

Paul was not perfect by any means; but, because of his consistent attentiveness and obedience to the Holy Spirit, he was able to call his fellow believers to grow in their own obedience.

His pleas were often based on his own testimony of Christlike conduct among them, such as in 2 Corinthians 6, where he beseeches the believers not to receive the grace of God in vain, but to walk in obedience to the Lord's commands. This is what he reminds them of concerning himself and Timothy,

*"Giving no offense in any thing, that the ministry be not blamed: But in all things approving ourselves as the ministers of God, in much patience, in afflictions, in necessities, in distresses, in stripes, in imprisonments, in tumults, in labours, in watchings, in fastings; By pureness, by knowledge, by longsuffering, by kindness, by the Holy Ghost, by love unfeigned, By the Word of truth, by the power of God, by the armour of righteousness on the right hand and on the left" (vv.3-7)*

Notice how much of what Paul lists here ties directly to the fruit of the Spirit. We see love, longsuffering, and kindness (the same word as gentleness) specifically listed, and one could argue that the products of the rest of the nine qualities of the fruit of the Spirit are seen here also.

Paul's point is that his and Timothy's conduct before the believers to whom he is writing not only serves as an example of how a Christian should (and can) behave, but also validated their message. You cannot call others to a higher standard than you yourself are willing to meet. Neither will you convince others of a truth you are not living out.

This is why our behavior as Christians is so important. Saved and lost alike, how others see us act will often determine whether or not they are willing to listen to what we have to say. That is why Colossians 3:12-13 tells us,

*"Put on therefore, as the elect of God, holy and beloved, bowels of mercies, kindness, humbleness of mind, meekness, longsuffering; Forbearing one another, and forgiving one another, if any man have a quarrel against any: even as Christ forgave you, so also do ye."*

When we are walking in the Spirit, choosing to obey the clear commands of Scripture and the promptings of the Holy Spirit, we will treat others with kind-hearted gentleness, as well as longsuffering and all the rest mentioned in this verse.

## *Forgiveness*

Notice that it takes a longsuffering heart, motivated by God's love to treat others kindly, forbearing and forgiving regardless of whether or not we feel our forgiveness or forbearance is deserved. The fruit of the Spirit will result in the kind treatment of others, which in turn will result in forgiveness, for we will not treat others with kindness, gentleness, or graciousness if we are harboring unforgiveness in our hearts.

Earlier in Colossians 3, we are told to "put off," or remove from our hearts, anger, wrath, and malice. *(v.8)* Those are the companions of bitterness and unforgiveness.

Although forgiveness is not listed in Galatians as a fruit of the Spirit, bearing the fruit of the Spirit will nevertheless require you to forgive, because an unforgiving heart is exactly the opposite of the heart of God towards mankind. Notice in Colossians 3:13 that we are to forgive *"as Christ forgave you."* This means that there is no wrong too great for us to forgive, for there is no wrong too great for Christ to forgive.

Dear reader, if there is someone it seems too hard for you to forgive, think of your own sin and how heinous it is in the eyes of God. Then remember that forgiveness will only take place when you surrender your anger, hurt, bitterness, and fears to God, *choosing* to forgive. As you make that decision to obey, He will empower you to forgive.

God has shown His gentleness to you and me in innumerable ways. When we choose to yield our will, our schedule, and our cherished "rights" to God, He will in turn give us a heart that responds to others with the unfailing gentleness He has first shown to us.

# 7

# Goodness

> *"But the fruit of the Spirit is love, joy, peace, longsuffering, gentleness, goodness, faith, Meekness, temperance: against such there is no law."*
> Galatians 5:22-23

I don't think it would surprise anyone to say that God would want us to be good. After all, God Himself is unfailingly, invincibly good; and it makes sense that His followers would echo that trait. But what exactly does it mean to exhibit God's goodness in our lives?

The Greek word translated *goodness* here has the idea of virtue or beneficence. The form used in Galatians 5:22 (*goodness*) only occurs in three other places, but the root word is used throughout the New Testament in the wider sense we use the word *good*. (i.e. good character, good day, good cheer, etc.)

We can glean much about what *goodness* is and what it looks like in our lives from a study of these verses. But first, it is necessary to point out that goodness is clearly a work of the Holy Spirit. Like any other fruit of the Spirit, it is not something that naturally occurs in our hearts and lives.

A quick glance through Romans 7 can dispel any notion that Christians attain some sort of "sinless perfection" upon salvation. After all, it was Paul himself who penned the detailed description of the Christian's battle against sin. He also penned the next chapter of Romans, which details the victory found in Christ: a victory that can only be accessed through obedience to the Holy Spirit.

So as we look at the quality of goodness, remember that it is not natural, even to the Christian. It will require a moment-by-moment obedience and surrender to the Holy Spirit and the clear commands of Scripture.

## PROVE AND REPROVE

*"For ye were sometimes darkness, but now are ye light in the Lord: walk as children of light: (For the fruit of the Spirit is in all goodness and righteousness and truth;) Proving what is acceptable unto the Lord. And have no fellowship with the unfruitful works of darkness, but rather reprove them." (Ephesians 5:8-11)*

Goodness flows out of the Holy Spirit's working in our hearts and equips us not only to *"prove,"* or discern, the things that are acceptable to God, but also to *reprove* those things that are not. The more fully we embrace God's standard of what is good, the better we will be able to spot things that do not align with that standard. This in turn allows us to avoid those things and to warn others about them as well. (Always remembering, of course, that the fruit of the Spirit is *gentleness* as well as goodness.)

Goodness is crucial to the health of the church because it is a prerequisite for godly reproof. Part of the Holy Spirit's ministry is to reprove the world of sin, righteousness, and judgment *(John 16:8)* and He does that in part through the goodness reflected by Spirit-led believers.

Reproof is neither fun nor easy, but it is necessary. I can think of many times over the years when a brother or sister in Christ has cautioned or admonished me about something I hadn't realized was even important, or pointed out a danger I hadn't recognized. When these fellow believers cared enough about me to point out behavior or thinking that did not match up with God's standard of goodness, they had a significant impact on my growth in Christ.

We cannot reprove others, however, if we ourselves are ignoring the Holy Spirit's call to goodness in our own life. Reproof without the foundation of Spirit-empowered goodness will not only fail to help your fellow Christian, but actually do harm instead.

Reproof without goodness is like truthfulness promoted by a habitual liar. The message itself may be true and right, but no one will listen to or believe it because the messenger does not *act* in accordance with that truth.

When our actions fail to exhibit the goodness we require in others, it causes them to doubt whether that goodness is real or attainable, or if it's even good to begin with. Many a young believer has had a root of bitterness spring up in their heart over some inconsistency between an older believer's words of reproof and their own actions. Effective reproof can only come from a Spirit-led Christian walking in obedience.

As members of the body of Christ, we are each responsible to walk in the Spirit, obeying His leading and yielding to the life of goodness to which He calls us. Then, God can use us to speak goodness into the lives of our fellow believers as we demonstrate that which we desire to see cultivated in their hearts and lives.

## FULL OF GOODNESS

*"Now the God of hope fill you with all joy and peace in believing, that ye may abound in hope, through the power of the Holy Ghost. And I myself also am persuaded of you, my brethren, that ye also are full of goodness, filled with all knowledge, able also to admonish one another." (Romans 15:13-14)*

These verses again connect goodness and reproof, but notice that in order to admonish, or gently reprove, one another, we must not have only a *little* goodness, (and knowledge, for that matter) we must be *filled* with it!

The Strong's definition of the word translated *filled* gives the useful pictures of cramming a net full of fish. That immediately reminded me of the account in the Gospels of Jesus telling Peter to let down the nets, after Peter and the others had toiled all night long to no avail. Yet, Peter chose to respond in obedience, if not faith:

*"Nevertheless at Thy word I will let down the net." (Luke 5:5)*

What followed was a miraculous catch, the nets full to the point of breaking, so full, in fact, that the weight of the fish threatened to sink both ships!

Think of how full those nets were, and then carry that picture in your mind's eye as you consider Paul's statement that the Roman believers were *"full of goodness."* We are to be filled to bursting, to overflow with the virtue and beneficence of God. Is that true of you?

There are many verses that speak to the fact that Christians are to be characterized by goodness: 1 Peter 3:16 mentions the importance of a good conscience and *conversation*, or manner of living:

> "Having a good conscience; that, whereas they speak evil of you, as of evildoers, they may be ashamed that falsely accuse your good conversation in Christ."

Here we see unity of the heart and actions: a sincere goodness springing from the Spirit-filled heart resulting in good actions. Genuine goodness will always be rooted in the heart and will always result in outward goodness. In other words, a good conscience will result in good deeds.

1 Timothy 1:5 also mentions the conscience, but notice what it is linked to:

> "Now the end of the commandment is charity out of a pure heart, and of a good conscience, and of faith unfeigned."

The "commandment" in this verse refers to Scripture, specifically those parts of Scripture that include commands to be obeyed. Thus the end, or purpose, of obedience to God's commands is partly to cultivate a good conscience.

There are two other characteristics of the fruit of the Spirit mentioned in this verse, charity and faith, both of which are to be sincere, genuine, springing from a pure heart. A pure heart is a heart cleansed from sin, a heart filled with God's goodness.

Goodness and obedience are inextricably linked, as are goodness, faith, and love. One cannot choose just one characteristic to live out: obedience to the Holy Spirit will bring forth the whole fruit, in all its fullness.

## WOMEN AND GOODNESS

There are four passages in the New Testament specifically linking women with this characteristic of goodness. This first passage comes from a discourse on caring for widows in the church:

*"Let not a widow be taken into the number under threescore years old, having been the wife of one man, Well reported of for good works; if she have lodged strangers, if she have washed the saints' feet, if she have relieved the afflicted, if she have diligently followed every good work"*
(1 Timothy 5:9-10)

There are a few things in these verses that might strike you as odd. If you find yourself stumbling over the age requirement, in particular, I encourage you to go read the whole chapter, which goes on to explain why the younger widows were excluded from being provided for by the church.

The areas of good works listed give a picture of a woman characterized by goodness: generous with her hospitality towards strangers, humble in service to other believers, gentle and helpful to those going through affliction, diligent in searching out ways to do good: that is the kind of widow God wants the church to honor with special care and protection.

This brings up several applications to us: could those qualifications be spotted in our own lives by those around us? Is there any widow in our local churches who ought to be shown special care and honor for a life exhibiting such wholehearted dedication to goodness? How can we encourage such qualities in our fellow believers?

The answer to that last question is simply to allow the Holy Spirit to cultivate goodness in our own hearts and lives, so that we can be used to influence others, both by example and by gentle reproof.

Next is a passage that really defines what a Christian woman is to be and do:

> *"The aged women likewise, that they be in behaviour as becometh holiness, not false accusers, not given to much wine, teachers of good things; That they may teach the young women to be sober, to love their husbands, to love their children, To be discreet, chaste, keepers at home, good, obedient to their own husbands, that the Word of God be not blasphemed."*
>
> (Titus 2:3-5)

Notice that the older women are to teach *"good things,"* and among the things they are to teach the young women is goodness. As a woman, I am to both *be* good and *teach* the next generation to be good.

A simple application for you and me is to ask ourselves, who does God want me to learn from as I grow in goodness; and who is there to whom He would have me teach His goodness? Regardless of your age and season of life, there is always someone both ahead of and behind you in the Christian life. God's Word calls us to be humble students *and* teachers, often simultaneously.

1 Timothy 2:9-10 is another well-known passage, this time dealing with what should characterize a Christian woman's appearance. Though verse 9 is where the focus shifts to women, I am including verse 8, which gives us the helpful context of the *"In like manner"* of verse 9:

> *"I will therefore that men pray every where, lifting up holy hands, without wrath and doubting. In like manner also, that women adorn themselves in modest apparel, with shamefacedness and sobriety; not with broided hair, or gold, or pearls, or costly array; But (which becometh women professing godliness) with good works."*

Notice that this passage makes reference to the attitude of prayer in the verse before: an attitude of holy reverence. It is in this same attitude of holy reverence that women are to adorn themselves. It is reverence for the holy God who calls us up to His definition of goodness that should motivate us to dress in modest apparel, soberly considering what we wear, seeking out and humbly submitting to the Holy Spirit's prompting concerning the appropriateness of our attire.

When others look at us, they should be struck by goodness, not worldliness, physical attractiveness, or even our sense of style. Much more could be said on this topic, but I think the best summary application for you and me is the following question: Does my choice of attire reflect *goodness*?

One of the most precious compliments to me is when someone tells me I look *wholesome*. That means far more than being told I look pretty or that someone likes my outfit. To have my appearance characterized by the adjective wholesome tells me that I'm on the right track in my attempt to reflect goodness.

One last passage dealing specifically with women and goodness is Acts 9:36, which is the description of Tabitha, also called Dorcas. This godly lady had died, and was about to be raised miraculously from the dead; but notice how she is described:

> *"Now there was at Joppa a certain disciple named Tabitha, which by interpretation is called Dorcas: this woman was full of good works and almsdeeds which she did."*

When we are full of Holy Spirit goodness, we will also be full of good works and what this verse terms *almsdeeds*. That word literally means *compassionateness*. It has to do with deeds done in compassion to the poor and needy.

As an example of this, we see later on in the narrative a group of widows weeping over the not-yet-raised Tabitha, showing Peter the coats and other garments she had made, presumably to meet the needs of these widows.

It is so easy for us, particularly in America, to get wrapped up in our own lives. We rush from one thing to another, focused on meeting our own needs and wants, instead of lifting our eyes from our routine to see the needs of others. But life in Christ is essentially a life lived for others, not for ourselves. As Romans 15:1 puts it,

*"We then that are strong ought to bear the infirmities of the weak, and not to please ourselves."*

This verse is in the context of things that would stumble other believers, but it shows clearly where our focus ought to be. Galatians 6:2 says,

*"Bear ye one another's burdens, and so fulfill the law of Christ."*

Like Tabitha, we are called to live with our focus on doing good toward others. In our own strength, life lived for others will feel like a cheerless and exhausting existence; but when we allow the Holy Spirit to direct and empower us, serving Christ by serving others will become more and more of a source of joy.

Of course, goodness is not just expected of women: the fruit of the Spirit is the same for every believer, whether male or female; but God does emphasize goodness as a quality that should specifically characterize Christian women.

Perhaps this is why the Victorian notion of women as being somehow innately good took such firm root in that period of history. Perhaps that is also why feminism has wholly rejected that notion, swinging the pendulum from one error to another.

Women are not innately good: the Bible clearly teaches that no human is. But goodness *is* to be a defining characteristic of the Christian woman's identity in Christ. The fact that our world fights against this is merely a confirmation of the Biblical ideal, for the world will always fight against that which is right in God's eyes.

## GOODNESS FOR ALL BELIEVERS

There are many admonitions to goodness in Scripture, such as 2 Thessalonians 2:16-17:

*"Now our Lord Jesus Christ Himself, and God, even our Father, which hath loved us, and hath given us everlasting consolation and good hope through grace, Comfort your hearts, and stablish you in every good word and work."*

The same God who loves us and gives us everlasting comfort and hope through His grace also establishes us in *"every good word and work."* It is not only our actions which are to reflect the goodness of God, but our words as well. Ephesians 4:29 says,

*"Let no corrupt communication proceed out of your mouth, but that which is good to the use of edifying, that it may minister grace unto the hearers."*

That which is good. Not only that which is simply not bad or wicked, but that which is positively good, that which is useful to build up, that which will minister grace to those who hear it. That is how our words ought to be. Our words, just like our appearance and actions, have a significant role in reflecting God's goodness to others.

We are also told to follow after, or pursue, goodness:

*"See that none render evil for evil unto any man; but ever follow that which is good, both among yourselves, and to all men." (1 Thessalonians 5:15)*

Following after goodness will cause us not to seek revenge, but rather to trust God to make all things right in His time. Again, at the end of a passage admonishing us not to seek vengeance, Romans 12:21 tells us,

*"Be not overcome of evil, but overcome evil with good."*

As we yield to the Holy Spirit's call to be filled with goodness, our desire for retribution will begin to fade; and as we take that desire captive to the obedience of Christ, we will find joy, peace, and hope in simple faith that chooses to trust God to do that which is right.

In the meantime, our refusal to render evil for evil, and our obedience to God's call to do good to our enemies *(Matthew 5:44)* may just cause our enemies to become friends instead. By yielding to the Holy Spirit and choosing to respond in faith, we are freed from the bondage of bitterness, hate, and anger. We are free to choose instead to bear the full fruit of the Spirit in our interactions, even with those who are our enemies.

Just a handful of verses earlier in Romans 12, we find the call to

*"Let love be without dissimulation. Abhor that which is evil; cleave to that which is good." (v.9)*

Notice again the connection between agape love and goodness. When we love sincerely, with Holy-Spirit-inspired love, we will truly abhor anything that is evil; and we will cleave, literally be stuck or glued to, that which is good. When we are walking in the Spirit, goodness will be as much a part of who we are as if we had glued it permanently to our hearts.

## THAT THE NAME OF CHRIST BE GLORIFIED

*"Wherefore also we pray always for you, that our God would count you worthy of this calling, and fulfil all the good pleasure of His goodness, and the*

*work of faith with power: That the name of our Lord Jesus Christ may be glorified in you, and ye in Him, according to the grace of our God and the Lord Jesus Christ." (2 Thessalonians 1:11-12)*

Paul through the Holy Spirit prayed that God would fulfil *"all the good pleasure of His goodness"* in the believers *so that* Christ would be glorified in them and they in Him. What does that mean for us?

Holy Spirit-led goodness leads to God's glory, but also to our glorification in Him. Thayer's definition of this Greek word is "to adorn with glory." In other words, Christ is adorned with glory when we live out His goodness through the power of the Holy Spirit, and we in turn are adorned with His glory as we reflect His character.

In a sense, we reflect both the goodness of God and His glory as well. This same idea is found in Ephesians 5:27 in reference to the church:

*"That He might present it to Himself a glorious church, not having spot, or wrinkle, or any such thing; but that it should be holy and without blemish."*

God is glorified when we reflect His character, and we are made glorious by the reflection of His gloriousness.

## GROWING GOODNESS

So where does the reflection of God's goodness begin? Jesus told a parable about a sower who went out to sow seed. As he scattered the seed, some fell on rocky ground, some on hard-packed earth, and some on good ground. Jesus explained,

*"But that on the good ground are they, which in an honest and good heart, having heard the Word, keep it, and bring forth fruit with patience." (Luke 8:15)*

Goodness begins with the Word of God, for that is the way God has chosen to reveal to us what He defines as good. As we saturate ourselves in Scripture, we will recognize what God calls good, and what He calls bad. We will see things as God sees them, because we have taken the time to get to know Him through His Word. Romans 10:17 tells us,

*"Faith cometh by hearing, and hearing by the Word of God"*

It is the Word of God that tells us what sin is, and what Jesus chose to do to pay the penalty each of us deserves for our sin. It is the Word of God that tells us to call on God for salvation. (Romans 10:9-10) And at salvation, the Holy Spirit enters into the believer and gets to work, preparing him or her to bring forth the fruit of the Spirit.

Romans also admonishes us,

*"And be not conformed to this world: but be ye transformed by the renewing of your mind, that ye may prove what is that good, and acceptable, and perfect, will of God." (12:2)*

As we spend time in the Word of God, the very ways we think and feel about life will be changed, transformed, and renewed by the truth of God. We will begin to see, among other things, that God's will is *good*.

2 Timothy 3:16-17 gives us a fuller description of what God's Word does:

*"All Scripture is given by inspiration of God, and is profitable for doctrine, for reproof, for correction, for instruction in righteousness: That the man of God may be perfect, thoroughly furnished unto all good works."*

Scripture will teach us what is true, warn us of what is wrong, bring us to repentance and restoration when we err, and teach us to be righteous, all in order to equip us for all good works.

Remember the account of Mary and Martha? Martha's complaint that she was doing all the work while Mary sat at Jesus' feet, doing nothing was met with the following statement:

*"But one thing is needful: and Mary hath chosen that good part, which shall not be taken away from her." (Luke 10:42)*

It's not enough simply to *know* God's definition of goodness. If we are to bear the fruit of the Spirit, we must choose the *"good part."* We must choose to spend time in the presence of God, humbly learning what He desires to teach us.

It's not just about Bible reading or praying through a list: it's about a relationship with God. That's where goodness begins and develops.

*"For we are His workmanship, created in Christ Jesus unto good works, which God hath before ordained that we should walk in them."*
*(Ephesians 2:10)*

# 8

# Faith

*"But the fruit of the Spirit is love, joy, peace, longsuffering, gentleness, goodness, faith, Meekness, temperance: against such there is no law."*
*Galatians 5:22-23*

As I write this, I have just been to a funeral. It was for an elderly man who was widely known as a man who loved God, loved the Bible, and loved people. During his memorial service, someone quoted Hebrews 13:7-8, which says,

*"Remember them which have the rule over you, who have spoken unto you the word of God: whose faith follow, considering the end of their conversation. Jesus Christ the same yesterday, and today, and for ever."*

You and I each have those in our lives whose faith in Christ God intends us to follow. This passage highlights the responsibility of those in authority to be ones whose faith others can follow, but the admonition to walk in faith is for all. Whose faith do you and I follow? Who are we in turn leading in faith?

## THE DEFINITION OF FAITH

You might be asking yourself, "What exactly *is* faith?" *Faith* has a broad definition in English, as it does in the original Greek. It could mean saving faith, or faithfulness to God, or to Christianity as a system of beliefs.

The Greek word itself, *pistis*, means persuasion or moral conviction, often used specifically with regard to our reliance upon God for salvation. This is a case where the Greek word itself does not shed much light on the definition of what faith actually is, but thankfully, God has given us His own definition of faith:

*"Now faith is the substance of things hoped for, the evidence of things not seen." (Hebrews 11:1)*

We often don't *see* God working in difficult situations, but faith chooses to believe that He is. We cling to the truths of Scripture and resist Satan's attempts to get us to rely on what we see.

For the Christian, the visible realities of life are just the surface: the invisible things, the Holy Spirit's unseen working in hearts, the warfare in the heavenlies, God's often miraculous intervention in our lives, these are the true reality. 2 Corinthians illustrates this:

*"For which cause we faint not; but though our outward man perish, yet the inward man is renewed day by day. For our light affliction, which is but for a moment, worketh for us a far more exceeding and eternal weight of glory; While we look not at the things which are seen, but at the things which are not seen: for the things which are seen are temporal; but the things which are not seen are eternal." (4:16-18)*

As children of the Eternal God, we live our lives with our gaze fixed steadily on the eternal. We cannot completely ignore temporal things—

we need to eat, work, and perform all the mundane necessities of life—but they are not to be our focus. Our eyes are on the eternal.

The other day, I was out walking by myself, trying to reset my mind before sitting down to write. Strolling briskly along, wrapped up in my own thoughts, I was startled by an insistent little voice coming from a nearby yard. A little girl I had never met had called out to me as I passed, inviting me to look at the "Little Free Library" her family had just helped her put up near the sidewalk.

I wasn't terribly interested in the books, but her persistence made me stop and examine the titles through the glass window. This led to a short conversation; and, as I walked onward, I resolved to find some books the girl might enjoy and drop them off next time I went by.

The book exchange itself would not necessarily have caught my attention, but the potential to influence a neighbor and point her to Christ did. My focus at that moment shifted from the temporal to the eternal, and that led me to take time for something I would not otherwise have even noticed.

## FAITH AND SALVATION

Of course, we know that faith is the starting point for a relationship with God. Lost in our sins, separated from God, headed for an eternity in hell, we could not even begin to pay the penalty for our own sins. That is why Jesus, God Himself, came and died on the cross, rising again on the third day in victory over death and hell. But unless we turn to God in repentance and faith, nothing changes. Romans 3:23-26 tells us,

> "For all have sinned, and come short of the glory of God; Being justified freely by His grace through the redemption that is in Christ Jesus: Whom God hath set forth to be a propitiation through faith in His blood, to declare His

*righteousness for the remission of sins that are past, through the forbearance of God"*

Christ was the propitiation, or sacrifice in our place, that purchased our salvation; but that salvation requires *"faith in His blood."* Saving faith is the belief that Jesus paid the full penalty for your sins through His death and resurrection. 1 Corinthians 15:17-19 highlights the importance of the resurrection to saving faith:

*"And if Christ be not raised, your faith is vain; ye are yet in your sins. Then they also which are fallen asleep in Christ are perished. If in this life only we have hope in Christ, we are of all men most miserable."*

The reality of the resurrection is foundational to the hope we have in Jesus. Without it, we not only have no personal hope of eternal life, we also have no hope of seeing our loved ones who have died trusting in Christ's saving work.

Saving faith believes not just that Christ lived, but that He died and rose again. From that faith arises the sense of hope and joy we have in the promise that Christ's victory over death and hell will be ours as well. Of course, belief merely in the *existence* of God is not sufficient, for as James 2:19 reminds us,

*"Thou believest that there is one God; thou doest well: the devils also believe and tremble."*

Satan's host of fallen angelic beings *believe* that God is God: but that belief does not gain them salvation. Saving faith is belief mixed with submission to God. The devils believe, but do not submit to God's authority. When we receive God's gift of salvation, we do so in repentance of our sins, acknowledging both God's definition of right and wrong, as well as His right to have authority over us.

*"For by grace are ye saved through faith; and that not of yourselves: it is the gift of God: Not of works, lest any man should boast." (Ephesians 2:8-9)*

The remarkable thing about salvation is that it is *God* who does the saving. We cannot do anything on our own to save ourselves or to pay for our own sin. Saving faith trusts the faithfulness of God.

## FAITH AND SANCTIFICATION

*"And you, that were sometime alienated and enemies in your mind by wicked works, yet now hath He reconciled In the body of His flesh through death, to present you holy and unblameable and unreprovable in His sight: If ye continue in the faith grounded and settled, and be not moved away from the hope of the gospel, which ye have heard, and which was preached to every creature which is under heaven; whereof I Paul am made a minister" (Colossians 1:21-23)*

The goal of salvation is not just to save us from the eternal penalty of sin, but also to enable us to become more and more like Christ as we live our temporal lives here on earth. Faith looks forward to the day when we shall stand before the Lord clothed in the righteousness of Christ, and seeks to live each day until then in victory over the world, the flesh, and the devil. Galatians 5:5 puts it this way:

*"For we through the Spirit wait for the hope of righteousness by faith."*

Faith gives us hope when it seems like our sin nature is just too strong for us. We can look to Christ and remember that He has already won our victory. It is simply a matter of yielding to Him and choosing to obey. As we do, God does His sanctifying work in our hearts, transforming us from the inside out.

This matter of sanctification begins with faith. The first chapter of 2 Peter reminds us that God has given us

*"all things that pertain unto life and godliness, through the knowledge of Him that hath called us to glory and virtue." (v.3)*

There is so much more to the first four verses of this chapter than can be easily summarized, but notice what comes after this assurance that God has given us all we need for life and godliness:

*"And beside this, giving all diligence, add to your faith virtue; and to virtue knowledge; and to knowledge temperance; and to temperance patience; and to patience godliness; And to godliness brotherly kindness; and to brotherly kindness charity." (vv. 5-7)*

The act of placing our faith in Christ for salvation was never meant to be the end of our journey: it is instead the beginning. It is the foundation upon which the Holy Spirit works to build us up in the righteousness of God.

## STRENGTHENING OUR FAITH

Godly character is built upon the foundation of faith, but we often feel like Jesus' words to the disciples could just as easily apply to us:

*"Why are ye so fearful? how is it that ye have no faith?" (Mark 4:40)*

Our salvation is not based upon the strength of our faith, but upon the sacrifice of the Savior on our behalf. Yet the Bible does say that our faith can (and should) be strengthened. This is often done through trials. While the first chapter of 2 Peter tells us about faith being the foundation of growth in godliness, the first chapter of 1 Peter tells us about the trying, or testing, of our faith:

> *"Blessed be the God and Father of our Lord Jesus Christ, which according to His abundant mercy hath begotten us again unto a lively hope by the resurrection of Jesus Christ from the dead, To an inheritance incorruptible, and undefiled, and that fadeth not away, reserved in heaven for you, Who are kept by the power of God through faith unto salvation ready to be revealed in the last time. Wherein ye greatly rejoice, though now for a season, if need be, ye are in heaviness through manifold temptations: That the trial of your faith, being much more precious than of gold that perisheth, though it be tried with fire, might be found unto praise and honour and glory at the appearing of Jesus Christ: Whom having not seen, ye love; in Whom, though now ye see Him not, yet believing, ye rejoice with joy unspeakable and full of glory: Receiving the end of your faith, even the salvation of your souls." (vv.3-9)*

This is a long passage; and if you're like me, you probably skimmed past it without really thinking about what you were reading. If you need to, read through it again.

See how the passage begins and ends with the foundation of salvation by faith? This emphasizes the fact that salvation is the foundation, just as 2 Peter 1:5 shows us. Salvation here is described as having been accomplished *by* God *through* faith. Then the subject of trials is addressed. There are several crucial truths about trials in these verses:

### Trials don't have to kill our joy

According to this passage of Scripture, we can rejoice in our future eternity with Christ in heaven even though we are *"in heaviness"* due to trials. As we have seen in our study of the previous characteristics of the fruit of the Spirit, the joy of the Holy Spirit is not dependent upon our circumstances. Christians in the worst circumstances often have the greatest sense of joy and peace.

## *Trials are necessary*

We don't like trials. In fact, we would probably go to great lengths to avoid any sort of trial or testing in our lives if we could; but that isn't how the Christian life works. God is constantly working to grow our faith, to strengthen and establish us through trials. Later in this same book, we find these words of benediction:

*"But the God of all grace, who hath called us unto His eternal glory by Christ Jesus, after that ye have suffered a while, make you perfect, stablish, strengthen, settle you."* (5:10)

Trials are a sign that God is at work. Instead of being discouraged when trials come, we can be encouraged by the fact that God will be with us in our trials, working all together for our good. The book of James also teaches this:

*"My brethren, count it all joy when ye fall into divers temptations; Knowing this, that the trying of your faith worketh patience. But let patience have her perfect work; that ye may be perfect and entire, wanting nothing."* (1:2-4)

Not only are trials valuable to our growth in Christlikeness, they are also valuable to our relationship with God. The suffering that God allows is intended to draw us close to Him in a way we never would have done otherwise.

All this is comforting, but it doesn't erase the pain or sorrow that comes with trials. When we are in the emotional, physical, or spiritual heaviness of trials, we can cry out in faith to God as the Psalmist did in the following verse:

*"I know, O Lord, that Thy judgements are right, and that Thou in faithfulness hast afflicted me."* (Psalm 119:75)

It is the faithfulness of God that allows trials in our lives for the purpose of strengthening our faith and knitting our hearts to His own. Trials are precious opportunities to draw near to God and delight in His faithfulness, however bleak our present circumstances may seem.

### *Trials are an opportunity to glorify God*

Trials are allowed by God so that our faith would *"be found unto praise and honour and glory at the appearing of Jesus Christ."* When we are going through trials, our first instinct is to think about ourselves; but while the strengthening of our faith is for our good, it is ultimately for the purpose of bringing glory, praise, and honor to God. After all, Jesus is the Author and Finisher of our faith: the saving and sanctifying work is all God's, so should the glory be! *(Hebrews 12:2)*

## FAITH AND THE FRUIT OF THE SPIRIT

By this point of our study of the characteristics that make up the fruit of the Spirit, you may have noticed that none stand alone, and faith is no exception. 1 Corinthians 13:1-2 tells us,

> *"Though I speak with the tongues of men and of angels, and have not charity, I am become as sounding brass, or a tinkling cymbal. And though I have the gift of prophecy, and understand all mysteries, and all knowledge; and though I have all faith, so that I could remove mountains, and have not charity, I am nothing."*

Later in the description of what Charity looks like in action, we are told that charity *"believeth all things." (v.7)* Faith without charity is just as impossible as charity without faith. The two are intertwined, as are all the characteristics of the fruit of the Spirit.

As we obey the promptings of the Holy Spirit more and more, we will find ourselves exhibiting more and more of *all* of these characteristics in our lives. It's not just a matter of picking one to work on, for they all are all part of each other, and all come from the same source: the Holy Spirit.

## FAITH AND VICTORY

*"For whatsoever is born of God overcometh the world: and this is the victory that overcometh the world, even our faith"* (1 John 5:4)

We all want victory over sin, but we often forget just Who it is that wins that victory for and through us. As the verse above states, faith is the victory that overcomes the world: faith that God has already won our victory, that He will be faithful to enable us to overcome sin in our lives if we but choose to obey. In the list of the "armor of God" in Ephesians 6, faith is likened to a shield:

*"Above all, taking the shield of faith, wherewith ye shall be able to quench all the fiery darts of the wicked."(v.16)*

While the "helmet of salvation" protects our eternal life and the *"sword of the Spirit which is the Word of God"(v.7)* enables us to fight back against Satan's attacks, the shield of faith is what quenches the fiery darts hurled at us by our enemy.

As mentioned already, Romans tells us that *"faith cometh by hearing, and hearing by the Word of God"(10:17)* In order to keep the fiery darts of temptation from doing their destructive work, we need to have hearts firmly grounded in Scripture.

We need to know what God is like, what He has promised, and how He has acted in the past. The more we know about God, the more faith takes that knowledge and applies it to our lives, quenching the lies of Satan by dousing them with truth.

There is so much more that could be said about faith, so many examples in Scripture of people highlighted by God for their faith, and of God Himself exhibiting His perfect faithfulness again and again; but I think a fitting conclusion for this summary study is a reminder from Hebrews 11:

*"But without faith it is impossible to please Him: for he that cometh to God must believe that He is, and that He is a rewarder of them that diligently seek Him." (v.6)*

If you are struggling to believe God in a particular area, remember that we cannot please God without faith. When we wrestle with the truth that God is good, even in sending us trials, or with doubting whether any good thing can come from our present circumstances, we can look to God in faith and *choose* to believe even if we don't *feel* like it.

Belief, just like the rest of the fruit of the Spirit requires an act of the will. We cannot have love, joy, peace, longsuffering, gentleness, goodness, faith, meekness, or temperance if we are not willing to obey God.

We must choose to believe; and, as we act upon that choice, refusing to let ourselves think as if God's Word were not true, God Himself will give us the power to believe fully, with heart, soul, *and* mind. Whatever our emotions might argue, the choice to believe is ours, and the rest is up to God.

*"I am crucified with Christ: nevertheless I live; yet not I, but Christ liveth in me: and the life which I now live in the flesh I live by the faith of the Son of God, who loved me, and gave Himself for me."*
*(Galatians 2:20)*

# 9

# Meekness

> *"But the fruit of the Spirit is love, joy, peace, longsuffering, gentleness, goodness, faith, meekness, temperance: against such there is no law."*
> *Galatians 5:22-23*

Meekness is a trait we don't often hear praised in our culture. In fact, the world's negative view of meekness has rendered many Christians confused as to whether meekness is a virtue or a weakness. According to Scripture, meekness is not a weakness. In fact, it is one of the ways in which a Christian exhibits strength. But what exactly is meekness?

The word here in Galatians 5:23 is part of a family of Greek words which combine the ideas of mildness, gentleness, and humility. This word and its different related forms appear throughout the New Testament as the word *meekness*.

Some translations of Scripture translate this word as *gentleness*, substituting the word kindness for the word translated as gentleness in verse 22. Having studied out the meaning of these two Greek words, it seems clear to me that the translators of the King James Version have rendered them as closely as possible to the meaning of the original Greek. Here's why:

*Gentleness* is an important part of the definition of the word in question, but the word *meekness* implies gentleness, along with humility and mildness. It encompasses the full meaning of the word. It is this combination of gentleness, humility, and mildness which flows out of a heart filled with the Holy Spirit. The foundation of meekness is trust that God knows what He is doing.

I often think that one of the best tests for whether I am exhibiting meekness is when I get stuck behind someone indecisive in a fast-food drive-through line. I'm sure you've experienced this before: you pull into the drive-through thinking it will just take a minute or two. After all, there is just one car in line, and you already know exactly what you want to order. You'll be through there in no time!

But then, one minute stretches to two, and the car in front of you doesn't move. As the minutes stretch on, your impatience grows... *Why don't they just order already?*

Meekness looks at life not with a prideful, "me-first" mentality, but with humility, gentleness, and mildness of manner. Meekness responds to situations like the slow drive-through with an understanding that God is in control of my schedule.

Instead of seething inside with impatience at the inconvenience to my schedule, meekness chooses to humbly submit to God's hand in allowing the delay. Meekness smiles a genuine smile at the worker behind the window and chooses neither to complain nor to fix the indecisive driver with an icy stare as they pull away.

## CHRIST'S MEEKNESS

Jesus Himself is our best example of meekness. While He did not shy away from boldly confronting sin and even physically driving out those who were polluting the holiness of God's chosen place of worship, He was nevertheless characterized by meekness. In fact, He described Himself as being meek:

*"Come unto Me, all ye that labour and are heavy laden, and I will give you rest. Take My yoke upon you and learn of me; for I am meek and lowly in heart: and ye shall find rest unto your souls. For My yoke is easy, and My burden is light." (Matthew 11:28-30)*

I think it is significant that Jesus chose to pair meekness with rest. You see, when we are not walking in the Spirit, our emotions are tossed about from one irritation or offense to another. We cannot rest, because there is always something to be upset about. Meekness chooses to rest rather than to fight for our pride's perceived "rights."

When we are tempted to give in to anger or irritation, we can remember that Jesus, who deserves all praise, honor, and deference, responds to *us* in gentleness and mildness when we have offended His *perfect* holiness. How much more ought we imperfect sinners to respond in meekness to those who offend us, knowing that we have been forgiven a far greater offense!

## BLESSED ARE THE MEEK

If we needed any further evidence that meekness is a good thing, we need only read Christ's statement in Matthew 5:5 which says,

*"Blessed are the meek, for they shall inherit the earth."*

Here is a commendation from Christ Himself, calling the meek *blessed*. That word "blessed" essentially means "happy." Thus, Christ is saying that those who are meek will be happy. This is quite the opposite of how our world paints the results of meekness. We are often told that if we don't stand up for ourselves, no one will do it for us. For the Christian, that is simply not true. Psalm 5:11-12 says,

*"But let all those that put their trust in Thee rejoice: let them ever shout for joy, because Thou defendest them: let them also that love Thy name be joyful in Thee. For Thou, Lord, wilt bless the righteous; with favour wilt Thou compass Him as with a shield."*

Our Defender is God Himself. We need not fear meekness, for it places the whole burden of our protection and vindication upon the perfect justice and omnipotence of God. We may not always agree with or understand the circumstances He allows, but we can rest secure and even happy in the truth that God is both sovereign and just and has promised to work all things for our good. *(Romans 8:28)*

That having been said, however, it is prudent to mention also that meekness does not mean refusal to confront sin; nor does it mean that a Christian should never make a stand against wrongdoing. Christ's example, as well as the teachings of Scripture, make that clear. Yet, as it is with Christ, meekness is to be one of our defining characteristics.

It has often been said that meekness is power under control. We are told by God that Moses was the meekest man on earth, (Numbers 12:3) but a quick read-through of the Biblical narrative shows us that he was nevertheless strong, even forceful, in his shepherding of God's people. However, that strength was kept under control and wielded in obedience to God. Meekness does not mean weakness: it means strength kept under the authority of God.

## RECEIVE WITH MEEKNESS

Meekness is a key characteristic for the Christian because it takes meekness to be teachable, specifically when it comes to the things of God. James 1:21 says,

> *"Wherefore lay apart all filthiness and superfluity of naughtiness, and receive with meekness the engrafted word, which is able to save your souls."*

As has been mentioned previously, saving faith comes by the hearing of the Word of God. In order to be saved, one must believe that God's Word is true. Meekness is required if one is to agree with God about his or her sin and the payment Christ has already offered for its penalty.

Meekness is necessary, if one is to repent from sin and place faith in Christ for salvation; and it is also necessary for our Christian growth. One of the ways the Holy Spirit helps us grow in Christlikeness is by *quickening*, or bringing to life, passages of Scripture we need to heed, whether for our encouragement, edification, or admonishment.

When confronted with truth from God's Word, we have a choice: yield to it or reject it. Pride responds in irritation or anger to the conviction of the Holy Spirit, often dismissing the convicting truth or making excuses as to why it isn't true in this particular situation. Meekness embraces the truth and turns trustingly from sin, acknowledging God's right to define what is right and wrong in our lives.

When we sit in church or read our Bibles or listen to a friend quote Scripture in response to something we say or do, are we receiving God's Word in meekness, or are we pridefully pushing it away or focusing on others who we think "need it more than we do?"

Holy Spirit-led Christians receive the Word with meekness.

## FLEE AND FOLLOW

The book of 1 Timothy was written to a new pastor in charge of a church in a rather difficult area. As the Holy Spirit directed, Paul wrote to young Timothy,

*"If any man teach otherwise, and consent not to wholesome words, even the words of our Lord Jesus Christ, and to the doctrine which is according to godliness; He is proud, knowing nothing, but doting about questions and strifes of words, whereof cometh envy, strife, railings, evil surmisings, Perverse disputings of men of corrupt minds, and destitute of the truth, supposing that gain is godliness: from such withdraw thyself."(6:3-5)*

These false teachers were responding to the truth of God's Word in the exact opposite of meekness. They pridefully denied the truth, *"consenting not"* to the words of Christ and the teachings of righteousness according to God's Word. These men were proud, ignorant, and argumentative about surface issues. They are called *destitute of the truth* and were focused on material gain.

In light of these false teachers and their contentious arguments, Paul instructs Timothy on how to respond:

*"But thou, O man of God, flee these things; and follow after righteousness, godliness, faith, love, patience, meekness." (6:11)*

Notice how many characteristics of the fruit of the Spirit are mentioned here. As we yield to the Holy Spirit's promptings, we will meet contentiousness and greed with righteousness, faith, love, patience (longsuffering,) as well as meekness. Colossians 3 gives us a similar list:

*"Put on therefore, as the elect of God, holy and beloved, bowels of mercies, kindness, humbleness of mind, meekness, longsuffering; Forbearing one another, and forgiving one another, if any man have a quarrel against any:*

*even as Christ forgave you, so also do ye. And above all these things put on charity, which is the bond of perfectness. And let the peace of God rule in your hearts, to the which also ye are called in one body; and be ye thankful. Let the word of Christ dwell in you richly in all wisdom; teaching and admonishing one another in psalms and hymns and spiritual songs, singing with grace in your hearts to the Lord." (vv. 12-16)*

Again, this passage mentions many of the characteristics of the fruit of the Spirit and shows us that meekness is to go hand in hand with compassion, humbleness of mind, longsuffering, forbearance, forgiveness, and charity.

As we meekly yield to the Spirit in these things, the peace of God will rule in our hearts, filling us with gratitude. We will in meekness receive the Word of God, letting it dwell in our hearts instead of letting it go in one ear and out the other. And with the Word of God dwelling in our hearts, it will naturally flow out of us even in our singing.

## ORNAMENT OF MEEKNESS

For women, this characteristic of meekness is especially precious, for we are told in 1 Peter 3:

*"Whose adorning let it not be that outward adorning of plaiting of the hair, and of wearing of gold, or of putting on of apparel; But let it be the hidden man of the heart, in that which is not corruptible, even the ornament of a meek and quiet spirit, which is in the sight of God of great price." (vv.3-4)*

This is yet another characteristic of the fruit of the Spirit which runs opposite to the ideals of our culture for women; yet God says that a meek and quiet spirit is precious, of great price in His sight. What is this meek and quiet spirit? It is no accident that these two verses are bookended by two commendations to wives to be in submission to their husbands.

Married or single, you have probably noticed that submission does not come naturally. Ever since Eve decided to take things into her own hands and act in opposition to God's command, women have struggled to accept God's authority structure.

I have heard it argued that the idea of the husband being the head of the wife is based on Old Testament law and is not relevant to today; but 1 Timothy 2 bases its teaching on the authority structure of the home and the church on creation, stating,

> "For Adam was first formed, then Eve." (v.13)

God created Adam first, then formed Eve out of Adam's rib and gave her to him to be a helper for him. Since creation, God's design was for the husband to be the head, and for him to protect, provide for, and cherish his wife.

Ephesians says that husbands are to love their wives as Christ loved the church and gave Himself for it. *(5:25)* Wives in turn are told to submit themselves to their own husbands just as the church is in submission to Christ.

Marriage is to be a picture of the relationship between Christ and the church; and, in order to fulfill that purpose, the husband must love sacrificially and the wife must love submissively. This obviously takes sacrifice and self-denial on both sides.

Note that the failure of one spouse does not excuse the other from fulfilling his or her own Scriptural role. Wives with unbelieving husbands are the context in which our passage in 1 Peter appears. It is there to encourage and admonish wives that their meekness in submission even to an unsaved, ungodly husband is a powerful tool in the hand of the Holy Spirit.

The wife characterized by the inner beauty of a meek and quiet spirit silently but eloquently pleads the truth of the gospel in a way that words could never do. Why? Because submission from a meek and quiet spirit is a mark of a heart transformed by the power of God.

As women, we are to adorn ourselves with the beauty that will never fade: a meek and quiet spirit. But meekness is not just for marriage. The single Christian woman also has a responsibility to adorn herself likewise with meekness as she interacts with the authorities God has placed in her life.

## MEEKLY RESTORE

Meekness is also needed when dealing with those who have fallen into sin. Galatians 6:1 instructs us,

*"Brethren, if a man be overtaken in a fault, ye which are spiritual, restore such an one in the spirit of meekness; considering thyself, lest thou also be tempted."*

Spirit-led Christians will find themselves helping their fellow Christians up when they have fallen into sin. This passage tells us that this ought to be done in meekness, with the realization that we, too, could fall into sin. This reminds me of 1 Corinthians 10:12, which says,

*"Wherefore let him that thinketh he standeth take heed lest he fall."*

We must never underestimate the weakness of our flesh. We are each capable of more grievous sin than we could ever imagine: the only thing standing between us and the depths of depravity is the grace of God. When God calls us to minister to a fallen brother or sister in Christ, we must always do so in meekness, wary of the pride that will set us up for a fall of our own.

2 Timothy also addresses the attitude of correction:

*"And the servant of the Lord must not strive; but be gentle unto all men, apt to teach, patient, In meekness instructing those that oppose themselves; if God peradventure will give them repentance to the acknowledging of the truth; And that they may recover themselves out of the snare of the devil, who are taken captive by him at his will." (2:24-26)*

Meekness does not excuse or enable sin, but approaches the sin-bound in humility and patience, taking time to deal gently with them while teaching them what God's Word has to say about their sin and the victory they can have in Christ. Meekness is unflappable in the face of bluster or insult and is constant in the face of inconsistency. It puts the love and mercy of God on display while also upholding God's truth and holiness.

1 Peter 3:15 points out that we must also use meekness in sharing the gospel with unbelievers.

*"But sanctify the Lord God in your hearts: and be ready always to give an answer to every man that asketh you a reason of the hope that is in you with meekness and fear"*

Meekness refuses to get pulled into a petty argument. It is never condescending or holier-than-thou, it simply gives a reason for the hope of Christ: a hope which should be on display in our lives for all to see.

Titus 3:2 also mentions meekness:

*"To speak evil of no man, to be no brawlers, but gentle, shewing all meekness unto all men."*

Like the passage from 1 Peter, this verse follows an admonition for believers to be in submission to their authorities. Throughout Scripture, meekness and willing submission go hand-in-hand. True meekness trusts that God knew what He was doing when He gave us the authorities in our lives.

Meekness is not just for our interaction with authorities, however. Notice that this verse tells us to show meekness *"unto all men."* All. That means there is no excuse for a Christian to respond to anyone else without meekness. Aren't you glad meekness is the fruit of the Spirit, and not something we must work up on our own?

As Christians, we are called to submit to the Holy Spirit in every area of life. As we yield to Him, He will give us power to respond in meekness rather than pride. That meekness will not only allow us to have a greater influence for Christ with those around us, it will also enable us to be teachable and grow in the Christlike character that God so desires to develop in us.

> *"But grow in grace, and in the knowledge of*
> *our Lord and Saviour Jesus Christ."*
> (2 Peter 3:18a)

# 10

# Temperance

*"But the fruit of the Spirit is love, joy, peace, longsuffering, gentleness, goodness, faith, Meekness, temperance: against such there is no law."*
*Galatians 5:22-23*

As we have examined each of the previous characteristics of the fruit of the Spirit, I have tried to show that none is intended to stand alone.

The fruit of the Spirit is one fruit, a unified whole of interconnected traits designed to work together, somewhat like the inner workings of a complex machine. Without one of its tiny teeth, a gear would be useless, and without just one small gear, the rest of the machine cannot function.

Thus we have seen love, joy, peace, longsuffering, gentleness, goodness, faith, and meekness each working hand in hand with the others as a seamless outflowing of the heart yielded to the Holy Spirit. We have seen how each of these traits is unnatural to our sinful flesh and can only be made part of our character by the Holy Spirit's empowering.

There is, however, a delicate balance: in order for the Holy Spirit to empower our obedience, we must be willing to obey and actually take steps to do so. It is *as we obey* that the power comes. This is where temperance comes in.

Temperance, simply put, is self-control. It comes from a Greek word that means to be strong in a particular thing, to be masterful. To be temperate means to take control of our thoughts, desires, and even emotions, to bring them under the mastery of the Holy Spirit. 2 Corinthians describes this process with regard to our thoughts:

*"Casting down imaginations, and every high thing that exalteth itself against the knowledge of God, and bringing into captivity every thought to the obedience of Christ" (10:5)*

Holy Spirit-empowered temperance applies the strength of the omnipotent God to our feeble attempts at self-control. As we obey, the Spirit gives us the power to master our thoughts, emotions, words, and actions so that we can bring them into obedience—not just to ourselves, but to God. As we have seen throughout this study, we do not have to do this ourselves: God gives us His own power with which to obey!

Temperance is like a child sent to tell his siblings to do something. If the child tries to stand on his own authority, his siblings will ignore or rebel against him. But if he utters the potent words *"Mom said..."* he will see a far different result.

When we try to take control of ourselves in our own power, we will ultimately fail. Somewhere, something will eventually snap out of line and we will find ourselves utterly undone. But if we humble ourselves and yield to the Holy Spirit's enabling, we will see greater victory than we ever imagined possible!

## IMPOSSIBLE?

James 4:6 reminds us,

*"But He giveth more grace. Wherefore He saith, God resisteth the proud, but giveth grace unto the humble."*

So often, our hesitance to obey is rooted in pride: we don't want to fail, therefore we don't want to even try. You may never have considered pride as the root of your fear of failure, but that's what it comes down to.

I have known Christians over the years who have disliked or even hated discussing the fruit of the Spirit because they felt it was an impossible list of virtues; and it is, but only to our flesh. Remember the promise of Galatians 5:16:

*"This I say then, Walk in the Spirit, and ye shall not fulfil the lust of the flesh."*

That phrase "shall not" has an extra negative added in the Greek which gives the idea of impossibility. If we are yielded to the Holy Spirit, it will be impossible for us to give in to the flesh! That is how temperance comes about. It is a result of willing obedience to the Spirit of God, maintained by His power flowing through us. By His power, He makes the impossible possible, and the inevitable impossible!

## BEARING FRUIT

2 Peter gives us another list of "impossible" virtues including temperance, but notice the promise at the end:

*"And beside all this, giving all diligence, add to your faith virtue; and to virtue knowledge; and to knowledge temperance; and to temperance patience;*

and to patience godliness; and to godliness brotherly kindness; and to brotherly kindness charity. For if these things be in you, and abound, they make you that ye shall neither be barren nor unfruitful in the knowledge of our Lord Jesus Christ" (1:5-8)

Temperance is one of the characteristics of Christlike character that causes our lives to be fruitful. It takes temperance to choose to spend time in prayer and reading God's Word when life is busy or difficult, or when you would rather hit the snooze button just one more time.

It takes temperance to choose to obey the promptings of the Spirit and walk away from temptation. It takes temperance to make your feet walk over to the stranger the Holy Spirit wants you to witness to, and it takes temperance to keep your mind focused on the sermon in church on Sunday when there are a million different thoughts vying for your attention.

In each of these scenarios, there is fruit to be borne: fruit of *"the knowledge of our Lord Jesus Christ,"* fruit of victory over sin and strengthened faith, and the simple fruit of God's hand of blessing on our obedience. Remember what Jesus said about fruitfulness:

*"Abide in Me, and I in you. As the branch cannot bear fruit of itself, except it abide in the vine; no more can ye, except ye abide in Me. I am the vine, ye are the branches: He that abideth in Me, and I in him, the same bringeth forth much fruit: for without Me ye can do nothing." (John 15:4-5)*

Fruitfulness is a part of the Christian life, one that cannot be had without the power of Christ through the Holy Spirit. A few verses later in John 15, Jesus tells us,

*"Herein is My Father glorified, that ye bear much fruit; so shall ye be My disciples." (v.8)*

Our purpose on earth is to glorify God. This is done when we bear *"much fruit."* Fruit can only be borne as we yield in humble obedience to the Holy Spirit, and allow the power of Christ to work through us.

## STRIVING FOR MASTERY

1 Corinthians 9:25-27 gives us the illustration of an athlete:

*"And every man that striveth for the mastery is temperate in all things. Now they do it to obtain a corruptible crown; but we an incorruptible. I therefore so run, not as uncertainly; so fight I, not as one that beateth the air: But I keep under my body, and bring it into subjection: lest that by any means, when I have preached to others, I myself should be a castaway."*

The prize we run this race of the Christian life to obtain is eternal. It is the glory of God throughout eternity and the never-ending joy of those words, *"Well done, thou good and faithful servant"* (Matthew 25:21) We limit ourselves now for the sake of Christ, who is even now preparing limitless joy for us to delight in for all eternity to come.

But here a note of clarification is needed. Do not think that the call to limit ourselves through temperance means that God delights in depriving us of joy. Just the opposite is true: God does call us to forsake some things, but only those that would harm us. After all, Psalm 84:11 tells us that,

*"no good thing will He withhold from them that walk uprightly."*

God, as a loving Father, calls us away from that which would hurt or hinder us, while at the same time calling us to Himself, the only Source of true joy and delight. Contrary to what our world teaches, a life characterized by temperance is neither cheerless nor dull.

Temperance is mentioned both in Titus 1:7-9 in reference to the qualifications of a "bishop," or pastor, as well as in 1 Corinthians 7:8-9, as part of the teaching concerning single women and widows. (The word *temperance* is not found in the 1 Corinthians passage, having been translated "contain," which fits both with the meaning of the Greek word and the context in which it appears here.)

My point in bringing these passages into our study of temperance is to show that it is a quality which is to characterize both men and women in their different roles. The man of God is to be temperate, as is the woman of God. There is no excuse for a Christian to be characterized by a lack of temperance—and yet, so many of us are.

We do not have to live in defeat: Christ has already won our victory; and it can be "accessed," so to speak, through obedience to the Holy Spirit. You *can* master that area of life that currently masters you, if you will make the Holy Spirit the Master of your heart and mind.

## IN CONCLUSION...

Which of the nine characteristics of the fruit of the Spirit seems the most daunting to you? My prayer is that this study has helped you see that the Christian life is a life lived in God's power. Nothing need daunt the child of God, for we have our Father's power at work on our behalf! All we have to do is humble ourselves and obey.

*"But thanks be to God, which giveth us the victory through our Lord Jesus Christ."*
(1 Corinthians 15:57)

www.ingramcontent.com/pod-product-compliance
Lightning Source LLC
Chambersburg PA
CBHW050306120526
44590CB00016B/2505